The Power of Repeated Reading

in Small-Group Instruction

Wendie Bramwell &
Brooke Graham Doyle

SCHOLASTIC

NEW YORK • TORONTO • LONDON • AUCKLAND • SYDNEY
MEXICO CITY • NEW DELHI • HONG KONG • BUENOS AIRES

Cover design by Maria Lilja
Interior design by Teresa B. Southwell

Photo credits: Cover (top), Chapter 2 (pages 33, 34): Andersen Ross/Digital Vision/Veer;
Cover (middle), Chapter 1 (pages 7, 8): ThinkStock/AGE fotostock;
Cover (bottom), Chapter 3 (pages 61, 62): Fancy Photography/Veer

ISBN-13 978-0-545-01209-6
ISBN-10 0-545-01209-0

★ CONTENTS

★ ACKNOWLEDGMENTS

We would like to thank the many teachers and administrators who have gently shown us how important it is to support the art and heart of teaching. We have held that principle in mind as we developed the strategies and suggestions in this book.

In particular, we would like to acknowledge Lassie Webster for her intrinsic understanding of what works for children and for her artistic ability to find ways to make activities meaningful. It is through her practical application of our ideas, that we were able to home in on what would be most useful to teachers.

We would also like to acknowledge the generosity of Andrea Zevenbergen for helping us understand and organize the research on dialogic reading.

We would also like to acknowledge Committee for Children for their important work in safeguarding the social-emotional development of children through their skill-based school curriculum.

In March 2006, we published an article, "Promoting Emergent Literacy and Social-Emotional Learning Through Dialogic Reading" in *The Reading Teacher*, the journal of the International Reading Association. This short article provided a framework upon which we developed this book. We greatly appreciate the encouragement and guidance we received from Virginia Dooley, our editor at Scholastic, throughout the development process.

A special acknowledgment to our families—Will, Meghan, Brendan, Dan, Emily, Anna, and Molly—for their support and understanding during the long weeks and months of developing, researching, and revising the material in this book.

~ WENDIE BRAMWELL and BROOKE GRAHAM DOYLE

INTRODUCTION ★

Teachers are facing a challenging time in this era of massive information about teaching strategies that are scientifically validated and research based. How do you sort out the recommendations and requirements? How do you make choices about what classroom practices to change? And most important, how do you retain your own passion for teaching, your own sense of creativity, and your unique relationship with the children in your classroom?

This book provides practical, accessible information that will help you do all of the above. It is about a research-based technique, called dialogic reading. Dialogic reading is a shared-reading technique that uses strategic questions during repeated readings of stories read to small groups of children. These questions open a dialogue between the teacher and children that continues at various points throughout the reading. The research on dialogic reading is compelling and comprehensive with impressive results in a variety of settings and with a broad age range—from 2- to 6-year-olds. Teachers have found the technique to offer a rich tool for meaningful language development in their classrooms.

Through our work with Committee for Children, we learned of the importance of integrating research-based techniques into practical teaching strategies when teaching social-emotional skills. (Committee for Children is a nonprofit organization that provides evidence-based, social-emotional learning programs to children around the world. We were part of the development team that produced curricula such as the *Second Step* Program and the *Woven Word* Program.)

A long-established appreciation of children's literature led us to the combination of using dialogic reading strategies while reading books with strong social-emotional content.

EMERGENT LITERACY, SOCIAL-EMOTIONAL LEARNING, AND LANGUAGE AND LITERACY SKILLS

This book is organized into three main sections: Emergent Literacy, Social-Emotional Learning, and Language and Literacy Skills. In the Emergent Literacy section, we introduce dialogic reading and provide guidelines on how to successfully organize your class into small groups for repeated reading. Dialogic reading has been shown to improve children's emergent literacy skills, particularly comprehension, vocabulary, and receptive and expressive language.

In the second section, on Social-Emotional Learning, we introduce the CASEL (Collaborative for Academic, Social, and Emotional Learning) categories of social-emotional competence. For each category, we focus on a children's book that reflects some aspect of the competency. A reading guide with sample dialogic reading questions accompanies each book. In many cases, we have chosen classic children's books because they are familiar to teachers and likely to stay in print, e.g., *Feelings* by Aliki (1984) and *A Birthday for Frances* by Russell Hoban (1968). We encourage you to select books that reflect the experiences of the children in your classroom. There are more and more outstanding books that portray children and situations in culturally sensitive and relevant contexts. In addition, we suggest classroom activities that will further enhance the skill in that competency area.

In the final section on Language and Literacy Skills, we demonstrate how to use the repeated readings and strategic questions of dialogic reading to address the additional key literacy skills of comprehension, narrative structure, and vocabulary development. Teachers are discovering that one of the powerful aspects of repeated reading using a dialogic reading approach is that they can teach more than one skill at a time. For example, by utilizing an intentional strategy to help build vocabulary while reading a story, teachers are integrating learning for students and increasing their comprehension of the text.

INCLUDING FAMILIES

Learning does not take place in isolation during the school day. Families are an integral part of the way children learn, what they learn, and how they feel about learning. Teachers, especially those of young children, have enormous influence on whether children and families move in partnership through the school system or if they feel isolated and in conflict with the school. Throughout this book, we present tips for ways to include families and suggestions on ways to involve families in the important work of educating their children. Handouts of important information to send home with children are included in the back of the book.

REFLECTING ON TEACHING PRACTICES

We offer opportunities for you to reflect on your own teaching practices through Teacher Reflection Sheets. These reflection sheets guide you through a process of thinking about teaching by gathering data about your own practice. This information will help you see ways in which you can make changes and refresh your approach to teaching.

CHAPTER 1

EMERGENT LITERACY

DIALOGIC READING

Shared book reading is an interactive way of reading books aloud with children that allows them to be active participants in the telling of the story. Dialogic reading, first described by Whitehurst, Falco, Lonigan, Fischel, DeBarysche, Valdez-Menchaca et al. (1988), is a specific type of shared book reading that involves strategic questioning and responding to children while reading a book. The questioning and responding occurs during three repeated readings of the same book to children in small groups. The adult prompts the children with strategic questions and careful responses that encourage the children to say more and eventually become the storytellers themselves.

THE CHARACTERISTICS OF DIALOGIC READING

★ **Is interactive**
★ **Features repeated readings of a book**
★ **Prompts dialogue through a variety of questions**
★ **Uses strategic responses to encourage language**
★ **Occurs in small groups of four to six children**

One of dialogic reading's critical characteristics is children's involvement in a conversation about the book throughout the reading. Children become active participants in the telling of the story instead of passive recipients. Rather than reading the story from start to finish without interruption, the adult pauses to ask questions and engage in conversation with the children who are listening. A dialogue about the story occurs, and then the reader returns to the text. This pause for dialogue, whether very brief or more extended, makes the experience more meaningful for listeners. Children have a chance to process what they have heard as they answer the questions. In subsequent readings, the questions begin to probe the text and illustrations more deeply.

The dialogue might clarify a character's motive or an illustration, center around how the story is similar to an event that happened in the class the previous week, or predict how a character will resolve her problem. Several children have a chance to chime in, and the teacher comments and helps turn those comments into a true dialogue that is grounded in the text. A robust conversation begins to come together. The conversation starts to blend with the storytelling itself as the children become comfortable with this structure. Their opportunities for expressive language greatly increase, particularly in the small-group setting. They learn that their voice is important and invited; with a chance to process a story's elements, they begin to understand narrative structure.

Several studies (Crain-Thoresen & Dale, 1992; DeTemple, 2001; Dickinson, 2001a, 2001b; Dickinson & Smith, 1994; Wasik & Bond, 2001) have shown that a crucial part of shared book reading is the verbal interaction between adults and children. In dialogic reading when teachers pause to check for understanding or ask children to relate the experience of a character to an experience they've had, children receive important feedback that helps them construct meaning. Furthermore, teachers learn when they need to elaborate or fill in gaps to build understanding.

For example, while reading Maurice Sendak's classic, *Where the Wild Things Are* (1963), a teacher wonders if the children understand the last line of the story about Max's supper still being hot. She knows the children love Max's adventures, the monsters, and his rumpus, but does the final line make sense? Here's an example of how she used dialogic reading to gauge their understanding.

Teacher: *How could Max's supper be hot?*

Connor: *His mom just made it for him.*

Teacher: *You think his mom just made it for him so it was still warm?*

Booker: *I think he came back a little too early. That's why it was still hot?*

Teacher: *Oh, you think he came back too early or just at the right time?*

Booker: *Too early.*

Teacher: *Oh, you think it should have been a little cooler. Rosa, how about you? How could Max's supper be hot?*

Rosa: *I think he's not even so hungry, when he was with the wild things, and he was sailing so much and then she gave him his supper.*

Teacher: *Hmm . . . If he was sailing so much, how could his supper stay hot?* [turning back to the beginning of the story] *Remember, Max was sent to bed without anything to eat because he was making mischief. But, then at the end of the story, his supper is in his room, and it's warm. If you wait a long time, what happens to hot soup?*

D'Anna: *It gets cold.*

Teacher: *Yes, if you wait a long time to eat hot food, it gets cold. When Max was having all of his adventures in the forest and on a boat, it felt like he had been gone a long, long time.*

Suki: *He was dreaming.*

Teacher: *Suki, you think he was dreaming. That he was dreaming about all of those exciting adventures. They felt like a long, long time in his dream, but it really wasn't very long. His mother brought him his warm supper while he was dreaming or imagining his adventures, and by the time Max found it, it was still warm.*

(Transcription from Webster, 2007 classroom reading)

In this exchange, the teacher affirmed children's verbal expression by repeating the child's responses and probing a bit further with a related question. (*Rosa: . . . when he was with the wild things and he was sailing so much . . . Teacher: If he was sailing so much, how could his supper stay hot?*) She continued weaving the children's responses with the questions she was posing to build the case for the understanding she was seeking from the students. (*Teacher: What happens to hot soup if you wait a long time? D'Anna: It gets cold. Teacher: Yes, if you wait a long time to eat hot food it gets cold.*) Furthermore, the teacher draws the children's attention back to the beginning of the story to refocus their attention on the detail of the hot supper. (*Teacher: Remember, Max was sent to bed without anything to eat because he was making mischief.*) The dynamic interchange allows both the teacher and children to benefit more than they would by a straight reading of the text without pausing for discussion. The teacher understands more about what the children comprehend from the text, and the children understand the story better.

SCAFFOLDING LANGUAGE

Dialogic reading is based on the theory that an important component of language development in young children is practice. We probably have all watched toddlers stack blocks over and over again, delighting in the tower each time they build it and knock it down. This methodical repetition is more than joyful fun; it's important practice of critical skills for toddlers. Young children enjoy and need repeated practice of the various skills they are developing, particularly language.

Dialogic reading gives young children many opportunities to practice language. In particular, its structure is built on scaffolded conversations with adults in small groups where immediate feedback is offered. With questions that you specifically choose for the small group of children in the reading group, you can help move them to the zone of proximal development (Vygotsky, 1978) where, with your help and the help of classmates, they can build new language skills. In other words, you can use your knowledge of your students to ask questions that help them extend their skills, moving children just beyond their current level. By breaking down a concept into a series of simpler questions, providing some elaboration of students' answers, and using other students' skills, you are able to extend children's learning. Your careful scaffolding allows students to move beyond what they could do on their own.

Fish is Fish by Leo Lionni

In Leo Lionni's *Fish is Fish* (1970), you have the opportunity to help children understand several sophisticated words that have important implications for the meaning of the story. In fact, if children miss the meaning of these words, they miss a crucial element of the story. In the beginning of the story, a minnow and a tadpole are best friends and enjoy spending all their time together. Their friendship is tested as the tadpole transforms into a frog and climbs out of the pond to live on the land while the fish is left in the water. Leo Lionni uses the word *inseparable* to describe the friends. Not many young children will fully understand the meaning of the word *inseparable*, but you have the opportunity to enhance their understanding by reading the word in a way that expresses its meaning. For example, you could use the illustration to show how the minnow and tadpole are smiling at each other. Repeat the sentence, "At the edge of the woods there was a pond, and there a minnow and a tadpole swam among the weeds. They were inseparable friends." Then you might say, "Look at how they smile at each other. It sounds like they had fun and did everything together. They were inseparable. *Inseparable.*" During a subsequent reading, pause and have a dialogue about the word *inseparable* and check children's understanding.

By emphasizing subtle clues in the text prior to a word's use, you help children understand the meaning of sophisticated words when they are used: "'Look' he said triumphantly." For example, by using dramatic pauses and emphasizing the word *look* in this passage, you can help students understand that the frog is excited and proud of the changes he has undergone.

In another passage, the frog describes what he has seen: "'Birds,' said the frog mysteriously." You can hint at the reason why the illustrations are distorted and humorous by emphasizing the word *mysteriously*. After reading the passage, pause to clearly explain the word *mysteriously* and to refer to the illustrations:

The frog is describing things in a way that invites the fish to use his imagination. The fish has never seen a cow, a bird, or even people. They are a mystery to him. When something is mysterious, it is difficult to understand. The fish imagines that a bird and a cow and even people look like fish.

(Show the illustrations, and have children read aloud the word *mysteriously* with you.)

"'Birds,' said the frog _____."

Also, by using a jealous tone when reading the following line, you can provide some clues for the reasons the fish decides to leave the pond: "'What else?' asked the fish impatiently."

In this example, you can see how you might scaffold children's understanding of sophisticated words. The extra support and the conversation you have with children help them construct the meaning—arriving at an understanding many children would not come to on their own.

Through dialogic reading's scaffolded conversations, adults can encourage children to say a little more each time. You might do this through eye contact, a pause in conversation, a probing question, a hesitation while reading a passage, or body language. For example, you might make encouraging eye contact and nod as a hesitant child is answering. Then, when the child appears to be finished, pause and continue to make eye contact and nod to try to encourage an elaboration. Or you can take a child's simple response to a question and restate it as a complete sentence. Even this simple action helps model more complex language and encourages children to say more next time.

REPEATED READINGS

Repeated readings are another defining characteristic of dialogic reading, and the repetition presents a perfect situation for scaffolding language—during each reading, you can check for understanding from the previous reading and extend the zone of proximal development gradually.

Of course, children love to read stories again and again, and research validates this practice. Children ask more questions and engage in more dialogue when they listen to repeated readings of the same story (Pappas, 1991). Questions during initial readings focus on understanding of the plot and clarifying comprehension. During subsequent readings, questions begin to probe deeper into character motivation and connections to the character and outside events. Children are encouraged to take on more of the storytelling by the third reading of a book. Study the following progression in questions using *Will I Have a Friend?* (1967) by Miriam Cohen:

★ Reading 1: *What is Jim worried about?*

★ Reading 2: *How does Jim make a friend?*

★ Reading 3: *What were you worried about when you started a new school?*

Children's comments also change over the course of the readings. After initially making sense of the text, they begin drawing conclusions and making predictions as well as participating more in the storytelling in subsequent readings (Phillips & McNaughton, 1990).

Children delight in knowing what is coming next—that on the next page the "creature" will finally relent and try green eggs and ham! We know the thrill that children experience when reading a favorite book again and again. Why is it so exciting? Think about the experience of listening to a piece of music for the first time. You might enjoy certain sections and find others jarring or confusing. A certain section might remind you of another song, while you might begin to lose focus during another part. Because it is an unfamiliar piece of music, you can't predict where it is taking you. After listening to it several times, you begin to anticipate the melody and enjoy the part that was initially confusing. This is similar to what children experience when they hear a story several times. After multiple readings, they are able to anticipate climactic scenes or a rhyming refrain. They are confident as they participate in the dialogue, and the familiarity of a favorite story, such as Dr. Seuss's *Green Eggs and Ham* (1960), offers children a safe place to practice new skills like retelling a story or trying out a new vocabulary word (Bramwell & Doyle, 2005).

As teachers, we respond to children's repeated requests to read favorite stories. Dialogic reading deepens that practice by adding a layer of intentionality. Research recommends that for repeated reading to be effective, the same book is read at least three times in a week (Whitehurst, Falco, Lonigan, Fischel, DeBarysche, Valdez-Menchaca et al., 1988); furthermore, questions asked during each reading should have a purpose as they uncover more layers of comprehension and connection. One of the benefits of the repeated readings is children's increasing familiarity with the story. By the third reading, the child has become the primary storyteller. Over the course of the repeated readings the balance shifts, so that the teacher talks more in the initial reading and the children talk more in the final one. Children's opportunities for expressive language practice in this activity are tremendous.

A VARIETY OF STRATEGIC QUESTIONS

Repeated readings in small groups with careful attention to scaffolding conversations sets up a wonderful environment for rich language development. Beginning the small group's conversations with a carefully chosen question is a critical ingredient. Most questions that teachers ask typically seek a *yes* or *no* response (*Have you ever felt like Corduroy? Ferdinand is happy smelling flowers, isn't he?*). All of dialogic reading's questions require more. In fact, part of the benefit of using dialogic reading is how the technique makes you more reflective about how you use language with children and more aware of your usual practice. (See Teacher Reflection Sheet 1: Language—What Do I Say?, on page 79.) Dialogic reading helps you become very strategic in the questions you ask and why. Throughout a reading session, you should use a variety of questions to address different types of language development.

The following questions refer to *Goodnight Moon* (Brown, 1947). To open the dialogue, you might use the following:

★   a WH prompt—e.g. what, where, and why questions

- ■   *What is the cow doing?*
- ■   *Where is the telephone?*
- ■   *Why is the quiet old lady whispering "hush"?*

★ an open-ended question defined as a question without a right or wrong answer

  ■ *Why is the little bunny getting out from under the covers?*

  ■ *What is the old lady knitting?*

★ a recall prompt to check for understanding and memory

  ■ *What is the little mouse doing in the bunny's bedroom?*

★ a fill-in-the-blank

  ■ *"Goodnight little house and goodnight _____."*

  ■ *"Goodnight kittens and goodnight _____."*

★ a connection question to relate the book's events to events in a child's life

  ■ *When you go to sleep at night, what do you say good night to? Tell us about it.*

The variety of questions described above is specifically targeting different language in children. A fill-in-the-blank is not looking for a lengthy response but whether a child can recall a word and use it in context. On the other hand, a connection question is looking for a more involved answer that demonstrates the ability to generalize a story event to a child's life. Being intentional and strategic about what questions you ask helps you set up a meaningful dialogue.

STRATEGIC RESPONSES BUILD LANGUAGE SKILLS

Once the child answers, you might respond in one of the following ways as these examples demonstrate:

★ Repeat the child's answer. This affirms the child's response.

  Child: *Chrysanthemum is upset.*

  Teacher: *Yes, Chrysanthemum is upset.*

★ Expand the child's answer. This models more complex language.

  Yes, Leo feels proud of all the things he can do now. Leo just needed time to bloom.

★ Gently correct the child's answer by modeling the correct word or phrase. This is a good opportunity to have the child repeat the correct word or phrase to you.

  I understand why you would call it a "handbrace." It goes around your hand. It is called a "bracelet." Can you say bracelet?

★ Validate the child's answer through body language, tone of voice, and/or words (for more information, see Figure 1.1: Creative Affirmations, page 28).

  Wow—what an interesting idea!"

  Then ask a follow-up question to continue the dialogue.

  Have you ever needed a little more time to learn to do something like Leo did?

The responses often overlap. For example, while repeating a child's answer, you might also be correcting a grammatical error she made and adding a few words to expand her response into a complete sentence. As you become more comfortable with the different techniques of responding, you will see that they flow naturally in conversation if you are watching for opportunities to use them. Families can also use these dialogic reading techniques in everyday conversation (for more information, see Figure 1.2: Helping Families Connect Through Everyday Conversation, page 29).

The techniques are meant to add tools to your repertoire so that as you engage in a dialogue with children, you have many options depending on what children say. A less verbal child may need a great deal of affirming, while you may have to add more sophisticated words to the answer of a very verbal child. These tools should not feel prescriptive. Instead, they should empower you as you find the words that work best with your style. (See Teacher Reflection Sheet 2: Affirmations, on page 82, for an interesting exercise about your own use of affirmations.)

Acronyms are useful in helping you remember the various elements of dialogic reading. For example, one group of researchers used **CROWD** and **PEER** (Whitehurst, Epstein, Angell, Payne, Crone, & Fischel, 1994):

CROWD helps you remember the types of questions to use.	**PEER** aids you in responding.
Completion prompts (see fill-in the-blanks, page 14)	**P**rompt
Recall prompts	**E**valuate
Open-ended prompts	**E**xpand
WH prompts	**R**epeat
Distancing prompts (see connection question, page 14)	

The Committee for Children chose the phrase "Question with CARE" in its *Woven Word* curriculum[1] to remember the key elements of dialogic reading (2004).

Question: Use a variety of questions (fill-in-the-blank, open-ended, distancing, detail)
With   **C**orrect   **A**ffirm   **R**epeat   **E**xpand

Mnemonics are helpful in remembering the structure of a dialogic reading conversation. Teachers often make up an acronym that works best for them. Try it, and see what you come up with!

---

[1] The *Woven Word* program weaves together key emergent literacy and social and emotional skills using children's literature as its foundation. Dialogic reading is used with books chosen for their social-emotional content, opening the door to conversations that connect with children's emotions and past experiences, helping teachers better understand students. Language is the common thread tying together the emergent literacy skills and the social-emotional skills, and dialogic reading helps bridge the two areas as it strengthens language.

SMALL GROUPS

Small groups are an important characteristic of dialogic reading. These meaningful conversations about a book occur in small groups of about four to six children. Studies (Morrow & Smith, 1990) indicate that children read to in small groups demonstrate better story comprehension than children read to in whole-class settings, and while researchers have not isolated the "active ingredient" in dialogic reading, it may well be small groups. The intimate setting allows you to be much more tuned into each student: *Who seems lost? Who needs more stimulation? Suki is not herself today. I need to talk to her later. Sajan connected this story to how he is feeling about his brother going into the army. Carlos was not able to offer any rhyming words to the sequence in* Hop on Pop. In a small group, a teacher can gain insight into students that is not possible in a large group.

Another asset of small groups is that you can shuffle their composition depending on your focus. You can put all of your strongest language students in one group for a few weeks, and then using some books with more complex language, you can push the group's comprehension skills with challenging questions. You can group the ELL students who are having the most difficultly and paraphrase stories for them, focusing on the main plot points and key vocabulary.

From the child's perspective, the small group offers a safe, comfortable place to try new skills. The opportunities children have to respond in a small group are tremendous. A child who would never speak up in a large group begins to trust her teacher and classmates and feels more confident in her skills. Children become better listeners in this intimate setting as well. They get to know you and their classmates better and understand the rhythm of conversation in a way that is impossible in a large group of twenty children. All of these aspects of small-group sessions are working together to build children's language skills. At the same time, children are developing their social-emotional skills. As children get to know their classmates better, they are able to play more easily in other classroom situations and build relationships. They are practicing some of the basic building blocks of social competence such as listening, taking turns, making conversation. It is easy to see how language and social skills overlap!

Working with small groups during dialogic reading's three repeated readings per book may be a shift for many teachers, including you, but there are compelling benefits that may motivate you to try this strategy:

★ Comments and questions increase and become more interpretive.

★ Motivation to read increases.

★ Vocabulary improves.

★ Children comprehend the text at a deeper level.

★ Teachers get to know their children better.

★ Children show increased self-sufficiency and independence.

The research on dialogic reading indicates that groups of four to six are optimal, but practical matters may lead teachers to begin by breaking their class into two or three groups of six to ten children. There is still increased opportunity for meaningful, more personalized interactions around the story in this larger group size.

Planning and Managing Small Groups

There are challenges to overcome in order to reap the benefits of the small-group sessions. When shifting to small-group reading sessions, you will need to consider the following four elements:

1. Space
2. Schedule
3. Management of Children Not in Small Groups
4. Group Composition

Space

★ Some classrooms are already set up with a separate reading area on a carpet or in a designated part of the room. The dynamics will be different when there are fewer children in the area, so consider ways of bringing children in closer to one another and to you during the reading session.

★ Hallways might provide the space needed for a pull-out group as long as there is adequate supervision for the children remaining in the classroom. If there is a lot of activity in the hallway, this might not be the best option.

★ Sometimes schools have small rooms adjacent to classrooms that are used by specialists, and these spaces might be ideal for a small-group gathering. Cozy spaces are conducive to quiet and reflective conversations.

★ Imagined or suggested boundaries might be necessary in rooms with few options. "Rope off" a small circle of the classroom that will become the reading area by using masking tape, ribbon, surveyor's tape, or colorful strips of fabric. Explain to students that even though the space is in the classroom, what happens within the circle is distinct from what happens outside it. Ensure that each child has a turn being part of the group that has time in the circle.

★ In crowded classrooms, it might be necessary to encircle chairs or desks in order to make a distinct space. The important thing is for you and the students to recognize that there is a reason for establishing this space and using it in a different way.

★ Curtains or draped fabric can be used to temporarily and gently define an area of the classroom that has multiple uses. For example, one teacher spread out a large blanket that was used only for small-group reading.

Schedule

To create time for small-group reading in your classroom, begin with an evaluation of your current schedule and then approach each part of the day by asking yourself reflective questions. (See Teacher Reflection Sheet 3: Schedule, on page 84.) This can help you gain new insights into ways to make changes that you might have previously assumed were impossible.

Most teachers do not have the freedom to set schedules by themselves. Lunchroom schedules must be accommodated, arrival and departure times are often complex, librarians set schedules that teachers need to follow, and outdoor time must be coordinated with other teachers. Yet in spite of all these complications, many teachers have made it a priority to work with small groups of children, understanding the benefits to relationships as well as language development that follow from these more immediate experiences. Consider the following suggestions:

★ Set aside half an hour three times a week to read to small groups. Recruit parents, assistant teachers, librarians, or community volunteers to come to your classroom at these specific times to read to one of the small groups. By using additional adults, all the groups will be reading at the same time.

★ Identify a block of time during the day when you can read, back to back, to all groups. For example, block off the hour and a half after lunch as Literacy Hour. Divide your class into three groups and read the same book to each of the groups. Assign related literacy activities to the children who are not in the small group.

★ Roll the small-group readings into the daily routines and set aside half an hour every day. Keep a running schedule of the groups. Track the children to make sure that each child hears the story three times. Assigning names to each group can help organize the system.

Management of Children Not in Small Groups

You may be uncertain how you will keep your focus on the children in the small group when there are ten or more other children who need your attention at the same time. Planning carefully and setting appropriate expectations are the keys to successful small-group sessions. Engage children who are not in the reading group with activities that relate to the story. Here are some suggestions:

★ Offer two or three choices to children who will not be in the small group. Clearly describe the choices and clarify what is expected during the time students are working on the task,

★ Have all materials prepared and ready for use before you begin the small group.

★ Encourage the children to seek help from one another rather than interrupting the small-group reading.

★ Engage the larger group in problem solving if there are repeated difficulties:
What are some things you can do if you need help spelling a word?
Who might be able to help with that?

★ Choose activities that will provide opportunities for children who need practice or additional experiences in a certain domain. For example, if several children in the larger group are behind in writing, prepare an activity that asks them to write about some aspect of the story. For emerging writers, ask them to draw pictures or work with a buddy.

★ Point out how helpful children are when things go well: *Thank you so much for working so quietly while we were reading.*

Group Composition

There is no "right" way to select children for groups, and what works for one teacher may not necessarily work for another. Be creative, flexible, experimental, and fearless as you approach this task. Think about the following criteria:

★ *Language* There are sound arguments either way for grouping children with similar abilities together or for mixing the group so you have a range of abilities. The important thing is to be open to both ways and willing to experiment with what works best for your particular group of children.

★ *Temperament* Sometimes children who have strong personalities dominate the group and prevent other children from benefiting from the conversation. Consider using the leadership skills of these powerful children to help with the group by assigning them a special job throughout the reading. For example, make a list of the children in the group. Ask your leader to help you by making a mark by the name of the child each time he or she comments or answers a question. Explain how important it is for each child to have a turn.

★ *Friends* You may need to decide whether or not you want to keep children who are already close friends in the same group or if you want to encourage them to expand their friendships with others. If you choose to keep them together, consider using the friendship as a model for other children by asking all the children to choose a buddy they can sit next to during the reading. Pose a question in which you ask children to talk to their buddies and come up with an answer together.

★ *Consistency versus variety* You should experiment until you find the right combination, but after some time, you may need to consider whether there are benefits to mixing up the groups. Sometimes the best choice will be to leave the groups constant throughout the entire year because you see continuous growth and benefits. Other times, you may sense that growth has reached a plateau and that the groups should be changed. Be alert to the clues so you can intentionally make a choice about how you proceed.

HOW TO BEGIN DIALOGIC READING

If you want to be more intentional about how you are using literature—and you especially want your English language learners to have a chance to boost their expressive language skills—you're ready to explore dialogic reading. Like many new skills, dialogic reading will become easier with practice. The structure and mnemonics are a way to get started (see pages 12–15 for a discussion of these elements). Soon it will become second nature and simply a part of how you interact with children. Here are a few tips about how to proceed:

★ To begin, think about how to schedule repeating readings during the day (see Teacher Reflection Sheet 3: Schedule, on page 84) and how to group your children.

★ Then do a few readings of a favorite book to try the technique. (See Handout 1: How to Become Familiar With Dialogic Reading, page 73, for specifics.)

★ Next develop a set of dialogic reading questions for another favorite book. (See Handout 2: How to Develop a Set of Dialogic Reading Questions, page 75.) You're ready to dive in!

MANAGING DIALOGIC READING GROUPS

The small-group repeated reading experience will encourage language! Be ready. Keeping children engaged and focused will help you manage the group. Here are some management tips:

★ Call children by name so it is clear whose turn it is to speak. You may also use a talking stick or similar tool.

■ Pause (and pause again) after asking a question to give more reluctant children a chance to talk.

- Be explicit in keeping track of who has had a turn so children can hear each other's ideas—for example, ask "Who hasn't had a turn to share?"

★ If a child offers a comment that is moving away from the story, respectfully re-direct his attention to the book. You might restate the question with more emphasis or point out the illustration that's related to the text.

- If the child is stuck on his tangent, validate his comment and offer to talk about it with him after the reading is over—for example, you might say, "I know you really want to tell us about your new puppy, but right now, we're talking about a pig named Olivia. I really want to hear about your puppy, and I hope you'll tell us during share time."

- If you feel that the tangentially related comment offers a teachable moment, capitalize on it! Use your professional judgment to decide what the child and the group need. The connecting questions in Reading 3 may invite children to share important events in their lives that they see as related. For example, if a character in the book is very sad, and the question asks about a time when you have been very sad, a child may talk about his dog, Harry, who died last week. This may, indeed, be the saddest thing the child has experienced to date, and he may welcome an opportunity to talk about it. The child feels comfortable enough with you, as the teacher, and the small group of his classmates that he has been reading with for a few weeks, to share something that is deeply painful. That openness is the power of the small-group repeated reading experience, particularly when using books with potent social-emotional themes. Be prepared for these conversations and decide how you will handle them. It can become difficult if every child begins sharing her dead pet story, but it might be an opportunity to explore sadness later in the day.

★ If a question generates no responses, rephrase it and wait a little longer. Ask children to look at the illustrations for clues. If necessary, break down the question into smaller parts that children can grasp.

- For example, in *Mike Mulligan and His Steam Shovel* by Virginia Lee Burton (1939), children offered blank stares when they were asked, "Why did Henry B. Swap smile in a way that was 'not quite so mean'?" The teacher acknowledged their misunderstanding by saying "I think this is confusing. Let's try to figure out what is going on."

The teacher used the opportunity to go back and find the other pages where Henry B. Swap smiled "in rather a mean way." The group discussed how Henry B. Swap was feeling when he smiled in a mean way. Then the teacher made it even more concrete by demonstrating such a smile: "Here is what I look like when I smile in rather a mean way. What do you notice about my face? What do my eyes look like? What does my mouth look like? I'm smiling, but it's not a regular, normal smile. I have another idea in my head that's mean. Who can show me what it looks like when they smile in rather a mean way?"

Then she returned to the original question and broke it down: "At the end of the story, Henry B. Swap smiles in a way that is 'not quite so mean.' When Mary Anne is stuck at the bottom of the cellar hole, what idea does the little boy have? Why would that idea make Henry B. Swap happy? That is why Henry B. Swap smiles in a way that is 'not quite so mean.' What does it look like to smile in a way that is not quite so mean?"

★ If a group has a large proportion of ELL children, preread the book and find pages that will be particularly challenging. Think of ways to simplify the text and paraphrase. Point to relevant parts of the illustration as you read.

STRATEGIES FOR SELECTING STORIES

There are no set criteria for what makes a book work well with dialogic reading, since an important piece of the success of the strategy has to do with the engagement of the teacher. If you love a book, that emotion will come across to the children, and they are more likely to become engaged. In addition, if you enjoy the story, you will be more likely to follow through with the repeated reading of the book. Develop a bibliography of your favorite books and select key social topics that can be teased out of the stories as the sample reading and discussion of *Where the Wild Things Are* on page 9–10 showed.

Use the following strategies to select stories for your small-group rereading experiences:

1. *Select several books by the same author.* Many authors who develop social-emotional topics in their stories follow the same set of characters throughout a series of books. The ongoing experiences of these featured characters provide students with a sequence of encounters and situations that builds on important literacy skills. In addition, authors often use phrases or repeated settings in the series of books that establish a familiarity for children. This helps them recognize attributes of the author even if the characters are different. Part of a classroom discussion can focus on comparing and contrasting books by the same author and/or illustrator.

Here are some suggestions.

Russell Hoban

Bedtime for Frances

Bread and Jam for Frances

A Birthday for Frances

Best Friends for Frances

A Baby Sister for Frances

Kevin Henkes

Chester's Way

A Weekend with Wendell

Lilly's Purple Plastic Purse

Chrysanthemum

Wemberley Worried

Miriam Cohen

Will I Have a Friend?

First Grade Takes a Test

Jim Meets the Thing

When Will I Read?

Rosemary Wells

Bunny Cakes

Timothy Goes to School

Yoko

Max and Ruby

Leo Lionni

Alexander and the Wind-Up Mouse

Frederick

Swimmy

A Color of His Own

It's Mine!

Tico and the Golden Wings

Fish is Fish

2. *Select books with cultural relevance and contextualized stories by authors from those cultures.* Classrooms today are filled with students who come from a broad range of cultures and backgrounds. The stories that once seemed to reflect typical experiences of children no longer work for many students in our classrooms. It is important to choose books with cultural sensitivity generated from within those cultures or with great sensitivity and knowledge of them. Use the stories as an opportunity to talk about perspectives, feelings, and understanding. We suggest the following books:

The Day of Ahmed's Secret by Florence Parry Heide and Judith Heide Gilliland

Angel Child, Dragon Child by Michele Maria Surat

Bread is for Eating by David Gershator and Phillis Gershator

Mama Provi and the Pot of Rice by Sylvia Rosa-Casanova

Baseball Saved Us by Ken Mochizuki

Mufaros's Beautiful Daughters: An African Tale by John Steptoe

I Hate English! by Ellen Levine

Roses Sing on New Snow by Paul Yee

Tar Beach by Faith Ringgold

3. *Read traditional fairy tales.* Challenge yourself to tease out the social-emotional themes in such stories as *Goldilocks and the Three Bears*, *The Three Billy Goats Gruff*, *The Three Little Pigs*, and *Rumpelstiltskin*. Consider looking at several different versions of the same tale and ask your children to identify the differences. In addition, select one author, such as Paul Galdone, who has written interpretations of several tales. Ask your children to identify the ways in which they can tell that the stories are by the same author.

4. *Look at poetry as another genre to get at social-emotional topics.* There are several excellent collections of poetry for children and some individual books, such as *Love That Dog* by Sharon Creech, that have rich content and imagery that lend themselves to discussion.

5. *Read chapter books.* Selections such as the Ramona series by Beverly Cleary have social-emotional themes that are covered over a period of time with the same characters. Chapter books are an important next step for helping children to build more sophisticated sequencing, recall, and comprehension skills.

DIALOGIC READING'S FLEXIBILITY IN YOUR CLASSROOM

As you transition into the routine of a consistent dialogic reading program, you'll begin to notice changes in children's conversations. The small-group work allows you to pay attention to some of the subtleties of the students' interactions and to become aware of social problems between children. For example, you might encounter a situation like the following: One student begins to overwhelm a friend with his attentions. He greets his friend by rushing up, lifting her up, and twirling her around. This causes the friend to withdraw and seek out other companions. The rejection makes the student feel frustrated and confused. He tries even harder and makes the situation worse. Their fragile friendship is jeopardized.

You can branch out and tackle a social challenge like this one during one of your reading sessions. The model below features Maurice Sendak's *Where the Wild Things Are* and shows how asking strategic questions can help stimulate a discussion about such a social situation in the classroom.

Teacher: *I'm curious about the very last line: "We'll eat you up, we love you so." Isn't that an interesting idea to want something so much you eat it up? It wouldn't be so good for the thing you love.*

Connor: *Except if it was some kind of thing you eat.*

D'Anna: *Like your sandwich.*

Teacher: *Oh, sandwich, please don't go. I'll eat you up, I love you so. That would make sense. But, let's say it's your friend.*

Suki:	*Oh.*
Teacher:	*What would that be like if it was your friend?*
Connor:	*You would be sad.*
Teacher:	[sighs] *Probably. How sad would you be?*
Connor:	*Really, really, really sad.*
Teacher:	*What would that be like to be a friend that was loved so much that you felt like you were being eaten up? Not for real. Anybody ever have that feeling? D'Anna, what is your thought?*
D'Anna:	*The friend would feel kind of scared.*
Teacher:	*You think the friend would feel kind of scared. You might feel sad or you might feel scared. Tell me if you have ever felt like somebody loved you so much that you couldn't leave. You couldn't do the things you needed to do. Do any of you recognize that feeling? Who would like to tell a story about that? Lola?*
Lola:	*My friend held me sooo tight and wouldn't let me leave.*
Teacher:	*You were with a friend and your friend didn't want you to leave. He was squeezing you so tight. I wonder if you could breathe. Did it feel like your friend was going to eat you up, he loved you so?*
Lola:	*Uh-huh.*
Teacher:	*Do you think that might be the way Max is feeling when he leaves the Wild Things?*
Lola:	*Probably.*
Teacher:	*Probably Max feels the same way. I was thinking there have been friends in our class lately who may want to change and sometimes play with other friends. And it's been hard to let them go. You want them to stay just the way they are. It just happens sometimes. It happens here in Max's story. His Wild Thing friends love him so they don't want to let him go. And it happens here in our classroom!*

The next time you notice the behavior, step in and talk to the two friends about the situation. By reminding them about the way Max felt in the story and linking it to the way Lola might be feeling, you can open the conversation in a neutral way, using humor and understanding in your approach. Ideally, the children will warm to your suggestion, and both of them will settle into comfortable changes in their choice of friends.

FAMILIES ARE PARTNERS IN DIALOGIC READING

Dialogic reading can open the door to a strong home-school connection. It can provide families with a particular activity to do with their child to help build language skills and to build a bridge between home and school.

The technique can be taught to parents in a straightforward manner. For example, you can hold a Family Night to introduce it, and duplicate Handout 3: Important Points for Families to Know about Repeated Reading on page 78 for families to take home. Emphasize to families that the most important thing is for the one-on-one time with their child to be enjoyable for both parties. The conversation can be about a book, or it can consist of making up a story together or taking turns talking about a topic—for example, *What I like best about winter*. The critical piece is focusing on the relationship and on language—asking questions, listening to responses, and expanding comments.

As families become more skilled at knowing what kinds of questions open up dialogue and how to respond to extend language, they will be pleasantly surprised by what they are learning about their child's progress at school. As children become more comfortable with this practice, they will begin to talk about what is on their minds. Important conversations begin to happen—important for language development and important for building relationships. Additionally, these conversations begin to happen in all sorts of places—while riding the bus, driving to after-school activities, cooking dinner.

If families can find a regular time to set aside for dialogic reading, the practice will begin to occur more easily. It might take some experimenting to see what time will work with everyone's schedule, but the event should be seen as a special time with a family member and not just ordinary homework.

If it is feasible for families to read the same books at home that are being read at school, the child will get a great deal of practice in comprehending and telling these stories. (See Figure 1.3, page 30, for suggested resources.) These multiple encounters with the same book give the child a great opportunity to practice developing language skills. It takes this repetition for children to be able to tell a story independently, and these additional practices at home are a great chance to hone skills. The child is the expert when the book comes home because she will have heard and discussed it several times at school. This creates a wonderful opportunity for the child to tell the adult the story. The family member can ask questions during the child's telling of the story that help connect the child's experiences with the book in a way that a teacher cannot. You probably wouldn't know, for example, that a student found some money and a hat at the playground and didn't want to turn the money into the lost and found, just like Jamaica in *Jamaica's Find* (1986). A mom or dad could have an important conversation about the child's experience by using the story of Jamaica as a parallel. This is simply not a conversation that would take place at school, and the powerful dialogue that occurs at home is rich in language and social-emotional content. Family participation makes that happen.

In these early years, it is even more important to invite families to be a part of their children's school experience. Dialogic reading provides a concrete way for them to be involved in what is happening in the classroom. A positive experience for both the adult and child early in a child's educational career will help solidify this partnership so that it lasts. Throughout this book, you'll see information to help create the home-school connection.

WHAT THE RESEARCH SAYS

A rich collection of studies attests to dialogic reading's effectiveness in promoting language development in young children. (See Figure 1.4: Research on Dialogic Reading, page 31.) Carefully studied for more than a decade with different populations of young children in a variety of settings, dialogic reading has a positive effect on oral language development—a cornerstone of emergent literacy—and a critical influence on later reading development. For example, a study of a six-week dialogic reading program with 3-year-olds from low-income families indicated that children who participated in dialogic reading showed significant gains in their expressive language which were maintained at a six-month follow-up assessment (Whitehurst, Arnold, Epstein, Angell, Smith, & Fischel, 1994). This is encouraging; even a short intervention can make a significant difference in students' language skills.

Expressive language skills are often an area of concern for teachers, especially those who want to boost the language experiences for students who are learning English. Repetition and small groups may provide for enriched conversations. Furthermore, oral language is the critical foundation students need for later reading. Research also shows even greater gains if families participate as well.

Researchers have found that when preschoolers with language delays participated in dialogic reading they spoke more, increased the variety of words used, and increased the length of their responses (Crain-Thoreson & Dale, 1999). See Figure 1.5, page 32, for information on dialogic reading and children with special needs.

Dialogic reading is most effective when families also participate in reading the same books at home that are being read at school by using the same conversational techniques (Whitehurst, Falco, Lonigan, Fischel, DeBarysche, Valdez-Menchaca, et al., 1988; Whitehurst, Arnold, Epstein, Angell, Smith & Fischel, 1994.) experience dialogic reading both at home and at school make gains in their language skills that are nearly double that of children who only experience dialogic reading at home or at school (Lonigan & Whitehurst, 1998). That's an impressive statistic to use when inviting families to be partners in their child's school experience. Dialogic reading provides families with a particular activity to do with their child to help build language skills and to build a bridge between home and school.

FIGURE 1.1: CREATIVE AFFIRMATIONS (See page 14.)

One way of increasing children's language skills is to provide them with experiences where they hear interesting words and expressions. Too often, adults rely on easy phrases and ordinary vocabulary when they talk to children. With practice and increased awareness, adults can stimulate children's interest in language. Begin by acknowledging children's accomplishments with something other than "Good job!" (Kohn, 2001). Children hear the same phrases so often that they tune out and the words have no meaning.

Challenge yourself to fit expressions to the situation and the child. Not everything a child does deserves an exclamation. Sometimes a quiet nod or a wink will communicate more than a verbal response.

The general suggestions shown below are followed by specific ways of affirming children:

★   Use children's names when you are affirming so they begin to associate positive attributes with themselves.

Ben, you are so quick.

Ernie, people feel like smiling when you are around.

★   Link the affirmation to other similar actions or behaviors the child has taken.

Sari, I remember you helped me carry these balls inside yesterday. Thank you.

★   Be playful with affirmations. Expand language by trying to rhyme affirming words with deeds.

What a twirl, little girl.

★   Reference the senses as a way of increasing awareness and vocabulary.

What a treat it is for my ears to hear you say such kind things to your friend.

Specific Affirmations

You can do it.	*Impressive!*
You remembered something important.	*What a clever idea!*
I can tell you're thinking.	*You look proud.*
What an interesting idea!	*That's a beautiful thought.*
I hadn't thought of that.	*Marvelous.*
Smart guess.	*Bravo!*
You're on the right track.	*Keep at it.*
You are almost there.	*Fantastic!*

FIGURE 1.2: HELPING FAMILIES CONNECT THROUGH EVERYDAY CONVERSATION (See page 15.)

Families have many opportunities to engage in dialogue with their children. These conversations build relationships and language skills—both are vital to later success—and when families talk about school with their children, it impacts students' expectations and aspirations (Shartrand, Weiss, Kreider, & Lopez, 1997).

Conversations over dinner are a great way to begin, since families are gathered at the end of the day and can debrief its events, but these conversations may also occur on the bus, in the car, during bath time, and so on. Barbara Meltz, a *Boston Globe* journalist, offers some pointers to help the dialogue flow well (2004):

★ "How was your day?" is a difficult question for a young child to answer. It requires a level of reflection, sequencing, and organizing that a young child cannot do. Instead, a question like "What was the most fun thing you did today?" or "What made you laugh really hard today?" works better.

★ Asking about a specific event or time also helps—for example, "Who did you sit by at lunch today?" or "What happened in the story Mr. Ramos read today?"

★ Emphasize the importance of social-emotional issues by asking questions such as "What kind thing did you do today?" or "Whom did you help today?"

★ Many children may not be ready to talk right after school. Bedtime or dinnertime may work better for a dialogue.

★ When families first see their child after school, acknowledging him or her is important— for example, "Welcome home. I'm glad to see you" or "I missed you today. You look a little tired."

★ If a child opens up about a sensitive subject, such as a classmate making fun of him or her or having trouble when reading aloud, families should try to withhold judgment and validate the child's feelings. As the child feels comfortable, the adult can begin to ask more questions and find out more. This important dialogue will help build trust and understanding.

★ Use the dialogic reading techniques of repeating, expanding, and validating to extend and encourage language.

FIGURE 1.3: RESOURCES FOR GETTING BOOKS TO FAMILIES

(See page 26.)

The following resources and ideas can help families get involved in dialogic reading at home:

★ Set up a lending library in your classroom so children can take turns borrowing the books that are being read. Ask the school librarian if you can reserve any school library copies for the period you are reading the book in the classroom. Children can even help set up a system for lending the books—for example, making the cards and decorating a chart that keeps track of who has which book and when it is due.

★ Arrange a class visit to a local library and invite families. Consider holding it in the evening if more families are likely to attend and turning it into a festival of books. Libraries are an incredible resource and should be celebrated! Encourage everyone to get a library card. Work with the librarian to reserve the books that are being read in your class.

★ Investigate funding to purchase copies of the books being read in your class for families.

■ PTAs, community organizations, and local businesses often look for ways to support collaboration between schools and families. Improving children's home libraries is a compelling case for many businesses.

■ Reading Is Fundamental has a National Book Program that motivates children, families, and community members to read together through book ownership, motivational activities, and family involvement in children's reading. Schools may apply to be part of the program and receive new books and literacy resources for children and their families without charge. More information can be found at http: //www.rif.org/about/nationalbook/.

■ The First Book National Book Bank provides new books to children from low-income families. You can find more information at http://bookbank.firstbook.org.

■ Various companies have special offers to give free books to children from time to time. The best way to access these is to do a Google search for "free children's books" and comb through the results.

■ Visit the Scholastic website, www.scholastic.com, for information on joining its book club. Click on "Teachers" and then "Teaching Resources" to learn more.

FIGURE 1.4: RESEARCH ON DIALOGIC READING (See page 27.)

Researchers	Year	Study Length	Sample Population	Variables Influenced
Arnold, Lonigan, Whitehurst, & Epstein	1994	4 weeks	Upper-middle-class 2-year-olds with parents	Expressive vocabulary; linguistic fluency
Valdez-Menchaca & Whitehurst	1992	7 weeks	Low-income 2-year-olds in Mexican day care	Expressive vocabulary; receptive vocabulary; linguistic fluency; linguistic complexity
Whitehurst, Arnold, Epstein, Angell, Smith, & Fischel	1994	6 weeks	Low-income 3-year-olds in day care (home and school)	Expressive vocabulary
Whitehurst, Epstein, Angell, Payne, Crone, & Fischel	1994	30 weeks	Low-income 4-year-olds in Head Start (home and school)	Print concepts; writing
Dale, Crain-Thoresen, Notari-Syverson, & Cole	1996	6–8 weeks	3- to 6-year-olds with language delays with parents	Vocabulary diversity; mean length utterance
Lonigan & Whitehurst	1998	30 weeks	Low-income 3- to 4-year-olds in day care (home and school)	Expressive vocabulary; mean length utterance; linguistic complexity; linguistic fluency
Crain-Thoreson & Dale	1999	8 weeks	3- to 5-year-olds with language delays (with parents or special education staff)	Once adults were taught dialogic reading, children in all groups, even those in a control group, showed improvements in mean length utterance and vocabulary diversity.
McNeill & Fowler	1999	9 weeks	4- to 5-year-olds with language delays with parents	Expressive language
Hargrave & Senechal	2000	2 reading sessions	Preschoolers with researchers in Canada	Expressive vocabulary
Heubner	2000	6 weeks	Toddlers with parents	Expressive language; parenting stress
Chow & McBride-Chang	2003	8 weeks	Kindergarteners in Hong Kong	Emergent literacy skills; receptive vocabulary
Fielding-Barnsley & Purdie	2003	8 weeks	Low-income 5- to 6-year-olds in Australia with parents	Receptive vocabulary; concepts of print; rhyming recognition
Zevenbergen, Whitehurst, & Zevenbergen	2003	30 weeks	Low-income 4-year-olds in Head Start	Use of evaluative devices in narrative

FIGURE 1.5: DIALOGIC READING AND CHILDREN WITH SPECIAL NEEDS (See page 27.)

Dialogic reading provides a framework for learning that is suitable for most children with special needs. Small groups and repeated readings are practices that allow you to focus more strategically on the strengths of individual children, the cornerstone of special education.

The following suggested practices for *The Story of Ferdinand* (Leaf, 1936) may benefit children with special needs:

★ Share background information on the story before you begin reading. Talk about customs, such as bull fighting, and explain how the matador uses the cape so the bull moves around him. Explain how people like to watch the bull and the matador.

★ Provide abundant opportunities for children to complete or repeat phrases and to practice with the sound and rhythm of the words: "'. . . would sit in its shade all day and smell the flowers.'" Repeat part of the sentence: "Smell the flowers." Then ask: "What did Ferdinand like to do?" The children answer: "Smell the flowers."

★ Use gestures, facial expressions, and demonstrations to extend the meaning of a story. For example, when reading the description of Ferdinand smelling the flowers, model taking a deep breath.

★ Introduce a variety of props to help deepen the understanding of the story. Bring in a flower, and let children practice taking a deep breath and smelling the flower, just like Ferdinand.

★ Assign students a special task during the reading that allows them to be a part of the story—for example, "Paula will put the flower in her hair, just like the ladies who are watching Ferdinand."

★ Ask the special education teacher to read the same book to the child during a different part of the day. Remember—repeated readings are a hallmark of dialogic reading.

★ Act out one or two key scenes so that children have exposure to an interpretation of the story. For a brisk outdoor playtime, ask the children to pretend to be the bulls who want to appear strong and fierce. Have them leap and jump and snort and paw the ground.

CHAPTER 2

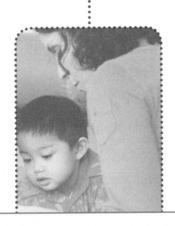

SOCIAL-EMOTIONAL LEARNING

WHAT IS SOCIAL-EMOTIONAL LEARNING?

For decades educators have been seeking the recipe for schools that would produce students who were well prepared for a successful life. Innovative and revolutionary techniques for academic achievement have held promise, only to fade after a few years. Research has provided guidance in many areas, but there is a lag between the studies that reveal important findings and the implementation of those strategies in the classroom. We are beginning to understand that how students feel may be just as important, if not more important, than how they think or what they think (Casas, 2001; Raver, 2002; Shonkoff & Phillips, 2000). In this current decade there is a movement to look more broadly at education and consider elements of learning that affect not just the mind but the heart as well. Efforts are underway to develop a better understanding of the synergy between learning and feelings. In education circles, this feeling realm is referred to as social-emotional learning.

Since 1994, CASEL (Collaborative for Academic, Social and Emotional Learning) has been a leader in advancing social-emotional learning and drawing the connection to school success. They have identified key characteristics of social development that are essential for successful students and provide a framework for classroom teachers.

SOCIAL-EMOTIONAL COMPETENCIES

★ **Relationship Skills**
  ■ *Communication:* Using verbal and nonverbal skills to express oneself and promote positive and effective exchanges with others
  ■ *Building relationships:* Establishing and maintaining healthy and rewarding connections with individuals and groups
  ■ *Negotiation:* Achieving mutually satisfactory resolutions to conflict by addressing the needs of all concerned
  ■ *Refusal:* Effectively conveying and following through with one's decision not to engage in unwanted, unsafe, unethical, or unlawful conduct

★ **Self-Awareness**
  ■ *Identifying emotions:* Identifying and labeling one's feelings
  ■ *Recognizing strengths:* Identifying and cultivating one's strengths and positive qualities

★ **Social Awareness**
  ■ *Perspective-taking:* Identifying and understanding the thoughts and feelings of others
  ■ *Appreciating diversity:* Understanding that individual and group differences complement each other and make the world more interesting

★ **Self-Management**
  ■ *Managing emotions:* Monitoring and regulating feelings so they aid rather than impede the handling of situations
  ■ *Goal setting:* Establishing and working toward the achievement of short- and long-term pro-social goals

★ **Responsible Decision Making**
  ■ *Analyzing situations:* Accurately perceiving situations in which a decision is to be made and assessing factors that might influence one's response
  ■ *Assuming personal responsibility:* Recognizing and understanding one's obligation to engage in ethical, safe, and legal behaviors
  ■ *Respecting others:* Believing that others deserve to be treated with kindness and compassion and feeling motivated to contribute to the common good

★ **Problem Solving:** Generating, implementing, and evaluating positive and informed solutions to problems.

from CASEL (*www.casel.org*)

Teachers are discovering that social-emotional skills do not always emerge naturally but can in fact be taught in strategic, intentional ways and reinforced by modeling, coaching, and practice. Many teachers find seamless ways to integrate social-emotional lessons into all aspects of their curriculum by the manner in which they present lessons, the expectations they set for classroom behavior, the way they themselves interact with students, and the guidance they give to pithy discussions about social issues that directly affect students in their classrooms. The teachers who are most successful in creating this classroom environment are those who have an understanding of the social behaviors they need to nurture and promote. (See Teacher Reflection Sheet 4: Classroom Climate, page 86). In other words, they have a picture of what those behaviors look like, and they present multiple pathways for students to acquire those behaviors.

Social skills, like any developmental domain, span a continuum. A 4-year-old will demonstrate skills that are different from those of a 12-year-old, yet the skills fall on a continuum of social development that in the broadest terms begins with a secure attachment that fosters empathy during infancy and develops into altruistic behavior in adults. For example, a 4-year-old who is beginning to show empathic behavior towards others may assist a child who has fallen down by patting a shoulder or bringing a favorite toy. A 14-year-old who witnesses mean spirited teasing of a fellow student, may step in to stop the teasing and become an ally to the classmate. Both behaviors are demonstrations of empathy, and there are specific classroom strategies that promote this kind of empathic behavior and other social skills that lead to overall social competence in students.

DEVELOPING SOCIAL COMPETENCE

A critical part of what children need to learn in kindergarten is social competence. They need to learn how to make friends and work together, how to take turns, listen, welcome peers, and join a group. These are all skills that help children make and retain friends and help them interact with peers in a way that is courteous and respectful. Furthermore, these skills bolster academic success by improving cognitive development, focus, motivation, and confidence (Zins, Bloodworth, Weissberg, & Walberg, 2004). It is these behaviors that make our classes gel or falter, and we need to make sure our classrooms are places where these skills are valued and taught.

RELATIONSHIP SKILLS: ENTERING A GROUP

Relationships are important to children. The ups and downs of friendship affect the way the class functions during work time. Children preoccupied with which lunch table will have a space for them cannot focus on sorting seeds by the speed with which they sprouted. Many students need some coaching on how to build relationships—from how to listen to how to negotiate fairly, how to compliment and how to assert oneself.

Many children find the transition to kindergarten socially challenging; they are with new peers in an unfamiliar environment. One area to focus on early in the year is joining a group. Approach the situation from both sides—entering a group and making someone new to a group feel welcome—so children see how they are complementary. They realize that they can be in either position, and they develop skills and confidence in both roles.

Books are a nonthreatening way to discuss social-emotional topics, and by using dialogic reading, you are also addressing critical language skills that in turn benefit social skills. Well-chosen books (see Strategies for Selecting Stories, page 22) can reinforce important skills and messages, such as welcoming behavior, and help build the skills of children who need some coaching on entering a group. In addition to the opportunities for learning that are presented by the small groups and repeated reading, children need a chance to practice the skills and review concepts that are introduced. For this reason, we have included classroom activities that enhance the skills in each competency area.

David's Drawings by Cathryn Falwell

In *David's Drawings* (2001) by Cathryn Falwell, a boy arriving at a new school makes friends with his classmates by drawing a picture of a tree. This simple story offers an opportunity to address both joining a group and including a classmate. Before sharing the book with children, spend some time with it yourself and brainstorm questions. For instance, you might focus on David's perspective in Reading 1 and discuss entering a group. In Reading 2 you can discuss his classmates' perspective and welcoming or including a peer. Then in Reading 3, you can encourage children to make connections. Some sample questions appear below.

Reading 1: David's Perspective—Entering a Group[2]

★ Dedication page: *What do you notice about David in this picture? How do you think he is feeling?*

★ Page 7: *The author tells us that David talks "shyly" on this page. When a person feels shy, what makes him uncomfortable?*

★ *What does David do when Amanda suggests that the drawing needs some grass?*

★ Page 9: *How is David welcoming the other children to help with his drawing?*

★ Page 11: *In the beginning of the book, David is always by himself. Now, he is with a group of his classmates. What do you notice about his face?*

---

[2] Many children's books do not list page numbers. For usability, our page numbers are calculated counting the first page with the story's text as page one unless the book already has page numbers listed.

★ Page 17: *How does David feel about the class picture?*

★ Page 23: *What do you think David's drawing needs?*

Reading 2: Other Children's Perspective—Welcoming and Including a Peer

★ Page 7: *When we say something nice about someone, like "Wow! You're really good at climbing," it's called a compliment. Giving people compliments is a way to make friends. Amanda gives David a compliment. What is Amanda's compliment? How do you think David feels when she says that?*

It looks like these two boys might want to join in the drawing, too. What can they say or do to join in?

★ Page 11: *What do you notice about the faces of the other kids with David? How are they feeling?*

★ Page 13: *David started the drawing by himself.* [Flip back to page 4.] *Now six other children are helping with the drawing. What did the other children add to the drawing?*

The children are all cooperating on the picture. What does it mean to cooperate? What would happen if they did not take turns as they cooperated?

★ Page 15: *What does Amanda say to David that makes him feel like he is a part of the group?*

Reading 3: Making Connections

★ Dedication page: *Have you ever felt the way David feels in this picture? Tell us about it.*

★ Page 3: *What is happening on this page?*

★ Page 7: *Amanda gives David a compliment about his drawing. What is a compliment you have given to someone? How does it feel to get a compliment?*

★ Page 11: *How does David feel? Why does he feel this way?*

★ Page 13: *What do you remember about this page? These children are cooperating as they draw. How do we cooperate in our class?*

★ Page 25: *What is happening on this page?*

Classroom Activities to Enhance Relationship Skills

Cooperative Art

Using *David's Drawings* as inspiration, facilitate truly cooperative art projects where each member of a small group contributes as the project is conceived, planned, and created. For example, have a box of mixed materials—pipe cleaners, toilet paper rolls, pie pans, egg cartons, cotton balls, and so on (for younger children, keep the materials simple in terms of variety and quantity), and tell the group to build something using everything in the box. You will need to facilitate the group problem solving and creating at first, to ensure that everyone participates. Begin by thinking of ways to help everyone play an important part. For example, you might assign different materials to different groups—pipe cleaners for one group and egg cartons for another. You might ask another group to do the painting at the end and have each member of the group use a different color. Such activities help relationships develop in your classroom and can lead to more welcoming and joining in groups in other, less structured situations.

Compliment Circles

Compliment Circles develop a culture of appreciation, inclusion, and observation and help build a positive classroom environment where welcoming peers into groups is normal. Build on the example in the story to introduce the practice. Explain what makes a good compliment and discuss how to receive a compliment. After introducing and practicing compliments, you can let the children decide when they want to have a Compliment Circle, or you can decide when the timing seems right for the activity to be a valuable experience. It is important that everyone in the circle receives a compliment and that the experience is positive for all. The process may take some skillful facilitation on your part to help children come up with meaningful compliments. Try to steer children away from material comments such as "I like your jacket" and towards behavioral observations such as "It was nice of you to share your lunch with me."

Vocabulary and Comprehension

In the story, Amanda offers David the compliment "Nice tree." It's a sincere and thoughtful sentiment using simple language. Use this opportunity to have fun with words. Have children brainstorm other, interesting ways to compliment his drawing using as many different words as they can think of—for example, "gorgeous tree;" "terrific painting;" "magnificent artwork."

Other Book Recommendations for Relationship Skills

Bourgeois, P. (1997). *Franklin's New Friend*. New York: Scholastic.

Initially, Franklin is afraid of Moose, his new neighbor, because of his size, but Franklin soon realizes that despite their differences, he has made a new friend.

Cohen, M. (1967). *Will I Have a Friend?* New York: Macmillan.

Jim's anxieties on his first day of school are happily forgotten when he makes a new friend.

Henkes, K. (1988). *Chester's Way*. New York: Greenwillow Books.

Chester and Wilson share the same exact way of doing things, until Lilly moves into the neighborhood and shows them that new ways can be just as good.

SELF-AWARENESS: FEELINGS IDENTIFICATION

An important piece of self-awareness is identifying one's feelings, a fundamental skill in social-emotional development. Many more complex skills such as emotion management and empathy rest on a basic understanding of feelings. Children at this age are capable of labeling emotions in themselves, particularly recognizing physical cues such as tears or clenched fists and contextual cues such as anticipating a birthday. It can be more challenging to help young children connect the internal physical signs with an emotion—for example, that "butterflies" in your stomach indicate nervousness—however it is useful to emphasize that feelings have signs in our bodies, such as a racing heart rate, rapid, shallow breathing, and sweaty palms generally indicate fear. Children can begin to make the mind-body connection.

Because feelings identification is such a fundamental skill, and it has many dimensions that can be added as students become more adept, it's important to emphasize it all year long. Keep in mind that different cultures express emotions in a variety of ways; talk to your students' families to learn more about how their cultures express feelings so you can be fully aware of the complexities operating in your classroom.

Some children may arrive in your classroom very aware of basic feelings and the words to describe them and are ready to think about feelings on a more sophisticated level. For others, the language of feelings is elusive. To help these students, find an entry point with any story—most stories involve some sort of change in emotions that drive the plot. Pause to ask children about a character's feelings and follow up with a question about the clues used to identify those feelings. Then have children show how the same emotions look on their faces and bodies. As characters' feelings change in the story, ask children if this new emotion is the same one that a character had earlier. Turn back to the page with the previous emotional state to clarify the change and to explore the contrast. This simple dialogue will work with almost any book and helps develop children's skills in feelings identification.

Feelings by Aliki

You can use *Feelings* by Aliki (1984) fairly early in the year to cover some fundamentals of emotion identification. It works even better with dialogic reading where children are learning that the small group is a safe place to talk about emotions. The book's pictures, dialogues, poems and small vignettes portray various emotions that everyone experiences—jealousy, sadness, fear, anger, joy, love, and others. Because *Feelings* does not have one storyline, choose a couple of pages to use in each reading, depending on the group's needs. For instance, if a child has lost a pet and is ready to talk about it, you might share the Whiskers story, which depicts one friend talking about her pet, Whiskers, who recently died, while the other friend offers comfort. Because having a pet die is often a young child's first experience with death and a common one for many children, this can be a particularly potent reading. To create the space for children to identify their feelings and to use language to process them through dialogic reading, ask simple questions such as the following:

★ *How does the girl feel? How do you know?*

★ *What does it feel like in your body when your heart is broken? Have you ever felt that way? Tell us about it.*

You can dedicate one reading to the "How do you feel?" vignette (page 31). After reading it, discuss some of the clues in the illustrations that indicate the emotion—for example, ask: *How can you tell that he feels shy?* Then help children make the connection to their own body's cues: *Show me what your body looks like when you feel shy. Tell me how your body feels.*

Devote another reading to "The Birthday" vignette (pages 26–27). Birthdays are such potent experiences for young children and bring up so many emotions as the story suggests. The captivating illustrations provide much to provoke conversation. Part Two of the vignette takes the perspective of a birthday guest, Bob, who makes a sundial for a gift. At first he's embarrassed that the birthday boy, Alfred, doesn't seem to like or understand his present. But then Alfred and several guests become impressed with the gift and the fact that Bob made it. Bob ends up feeling proud. This short scenario covers important territory for young children. Start a dialogue with questions such as the following:

★ *Have you ever been embarrassed about a present you gave? Tell us about it.*

★ *How did Alfred feel when he first opened the sundial?*

★ *When you receive a gift, what do you say? Why do we say that?*

★ *Why is Bob proud? When have you felt proud?*

The story continues to unfold with many entry points for relevant dialogic reading discussions that cover the important territory of emotion identification, so you can select the ones that are most applicable to each group.

Classroom Activities to Enhance Self-Awareness Identification

Feelings Chart

After doing several readings of *Feelings*, introduce a Feelings Chart showing faces with different emotions labeled. Give each child a card with his or her name on it. Ask each child how he or she is feeling, as the last picture on page 31 of *Feelings* does, and help each one place his or her name beside the corresponding feeling on the chart. This activity makes labeling one's own feelings concrete and gives children language for their emotions.

The Feelings Chart can become part of the classroom from this point on. As children arrive each day, have them visit the Feelings Chart to place their name cards next to the appropriate feeling they are having. At various points during the day or when children request it, call for a feelings check so children can reassess their feelings and move their names if needed. During the feelings check, be an empathetic listener as children describe their emotions. Always turn your body toward them and call them by name. Give children meaningful eye contact to validate their feelings. They can add emotions to the chart as the year progresses, and they become more familiar with feelings and interesting vocabulary words.

Feelings Collage

Put out dozens of magazines and a large roll of butcher paper. Label the paper with an emotion such as "surprised." Then have children make a feelings collage by drawing or using the magazines to find faces and bodies that show surprised expressions. Then initiate a discussion about what is common among the faces and bodies. Repeat this activity with different emotions on different days. If space permits, keep the older collages displayed as new ones are added so that children can notice the differences among them.

Vocabulary and Comprehension

Pages 26–27 of *Feelings* offers a vehicle to discuss the powerful and often unfamiliar idea of moods. Young children experience mood changes but may not know this is a universal phenomenon. Explaining and naming this experience is helpful. Use this Birthday vignette to talk about moods and what each one feels like. A feeling is strong but short-lasting, whereas a mood is not as strong and might stick with us for several hours or days. *Alexander and the Terrible, Horrible, No Good, Very Bad Day* (Viorst, 1972), of course, gives us a classic literary example of what a bad mood is! Ask children to think about different colors and what moods they convey. Similarly, play various music selections and ask children which moods it reminds them of.

Other Book Recommendations for Self-Awareness

Cain, B. (2001). *Double-Dip Feelings: Stories to Help Children Understand Emotions.*
Washington, D.C: Magination Press.
    A series of familiar situations illustrate the uncomfortable experience of having two feelings
    at the same time.
Cain, J. (2000). *The Way I Feel*. Seattle: Parenting Press.
    Illustrations and rhyming text portray children experiencing a range of emotions,
    including frustration, shyness, jealousy, and pride.

Robberecht, T. (2003). *Angry Dragon*. New York: Houghton Mifflin.

A young boy is sometimes so angry that he becomes a dragon, turning red, spitting out angry words, and destroying everything in his path. Later he turns back into a boy and can feel his parents' love again. This book vividly describes the physical signs of anger and helps children make the connection between the internal signs and the labeling of the emotion.

SOCIAL AWARENESS: PERSPECTIVE-TAKING

Socially competent children have the ability to identify and understand the thoughts and feelings of others. They are able to see situations from another's perspective and to understand the feelings that would accompany the experience of that person.

For a number of years, it has been a common practice to encourage children to explore their identity, build self-esteem, and find creative self-expression. While it is important for children to have the freedom to learn and develop their identity in a warm and nurturing environment, they also need gentle boundaries to learn what it means to live with the needs, demands, and dreams of other people. When children are so preoccupied with their own experiences, they can lose sight of the perspective and experiences of others. Simple social rules help children build an understanding of how to respect the perspective of others and how to navigate in a world with other people. The classroom is an ideal environment to teach social awareness and to reinforce the behaviors that lead to successful social relationships.

Carefully select books that match the social challenges that students in your classroom are facing. For example, you may notice a change in behavior in one of your students at about the time a sibling is celebrating a birthday. The child may begin to push in front of the other students in line, plop down in front of you during story time, and interrupt other children by talking out of turn. In a situation like this, read *A Birthday for Frances* (Hoban, 1968) to stimulate a discussion around feelings that arise when someone else is celebrating a birthday and receiving a lot of attention.

A Birthday for Frances by Russell Hoban

Russell and Lillian Hoban's Frances stories are some of our favorites, and the birthday story is a perfect conversation opener to help children with their conflicted feelings. In this story, Frances's little sister, Gloria, is about to celebrate her birthday. Frances fluctuates between feeling generous and feeling jealous.

43

Reading 1: Frances's Perspective

★ Page 7: *How does Frances feel when she says, "Your birthday is always the one that is not now"?*

★ Page 8: *What does Frances do that shows she is jealous of Gloria because it is her birthday?*

★ Page 13: *Why is Frances crying?*

★ Page 17: *Why did Frances's father ask, "You would not eat Gloria's Chompo Bar would you?" How was Frances feeling?*

★ Pages 20–23: *How do Frances and Albert feel about little sisters?*

★ Page 27: *How do you think Frances feels when Gloria says she is sorry for hiding her sand pail and shovel last year?*

Reading 2: Gloria's Perspective

★ Page 8: *Why is Gloria drawing pretty flowers, rainbows, and happy trees? Why did Gloria say, "Mean Frances"?*

★ Page 17: *Why is a Chompo Bar a good gift for Gloria?*

★ Page 27: *Why does Gloria want to tell her wish? Why does Gloria apologize for hiding the pail and shovel?*

Reading 3: Making Connections

★ Page 5: *Frances has an imaginary friend named Alice. Why does Frances have an imaginary friend? Have you ever had an imaginary friend?*

★ Page 15: *Have you ever given a gift to someone that you really wanted to keep for yourself? What did that feel like? What did you do?*

★ Page 22: *Frances and Albert had many things to say about their feelings for little brothers and sisters. Do you sometimes feel this way about your little brother or sister? Tell us about it.*

★ Page 27: *How do you feel when you apologize for something you said or did? How does it feel when someone apologizes to you?*

Classroom Activities to Enhance Social Awareness

Walk a Mile in My Shoes Story Game

The purpose of this game is to increase children's awareness of the experiences of different people using shoes as a concrete way of focusing attention.

Assemble a collection of shoes of all sizes and all styles. Include sports shoes, ballet shoes, working boots, slippers, baby shoes, ordinary day-to-day shoes, and shoes from various cultures. Gather the children in a circle and explain that you are going to create a story about the person who wore each pair of shoes. Select one pair to begin. Pass the pair of shoes around the circle of children while everyone says the rhyme below together. Whoever holds the shoes at the last word of the rhyme gets to start the story.

> *Tell me, tell me, mystery shoe,*
>
> *Where have you been, and what did you do?*
>
> *Did you run fast, did you walk slow?*
>
> *Tell me, tell me, where did you go?*

Model the first story so that children have an understanding of the qualities they should be thinking about. For example, holding a pair of children's soccer shoes, tell children the following:

> *These shoes belonged to Jake. Jake wore them when he played soccer with his neighborhood friends. Jake was not the best player on the team, but he had one spectacular game where he scored the winning goal. Right here on the toe of his shoe you can see where Jake kicked the ball that went past the goalie, right into the net. Jake will always remember how he felt when the team started cheering for him and patting him on the back. He felt proud. He kept these shoes until he graduated from college.*

To prompt the children to create an imaginary person, ask them the following questions:

★ *Do you have a name for your person?*

★ *When do you think your person wore the shoes?*

★ *Why did your person choose these shoes?*

★ *Do you know anyone who has shoes like these?*

Same Words, Different Meaning

The purpose of this activity is to help children become aware of how the same words can convey a different meaning, depending on the tone of voice, body language, and facial expression. Children who only listen to the words will miss important social clues about the intended meaning. Alerting children to attend to the broad array of social clues will broaden their perspective of social situations and give them skills to interpret situations accurately and respond thoughtfully.

Choose from the scenarios below, or create your own situations to match the experiences of your students. For each scenario, select two children. Explain to each child what the intended meaning of his or her words and phrases are and then ask that child to say the sentence, using tone of voice, facial expressions, and gestures to convey the meaning to the rest of the class.

The children observing will be looking for clues that tell them how the speakers felt when they were saying the words. After each demonstration, ask the observer children what they saw. Details are important! Record their responses, and at the end of the activity, summarize the number of ways children gathered the information to make meaning of the words.

Happy Birthday, Gloria.

- *jealous, sad, left out*

- *loving, generous, happy*

I have a new baby brother.

- *jealous, sad, left out*

- *loving, generous, happy*

My neighbor has a new dog.

- *excited, has fun with the dog, gets to see the dog every day*

- *worried, afraid the dog will bite, mad that the dog barks all night*

We had pizza for dinner last night.

- *loves pizza, excited, happy*

- *dislikes gooey cheese, pizza is brother's favorite but not mine, really disappointed whenever they have pizza*

My tooth is loose.

- *excited, feels grown up, can't wait for it to fall out*

- *worries, feels like his or her body is falling apart, dislikes blood, scared*

My friend built a tower using all the blocks.

- *proud of friend, admires the accomplishments, thinks it is great*

- *complains that all the blocks are gone, upset that friend is showing off and didn't let anyone else help*

Vocabulary and Comprehension

Russell and Lillian Hoban's books about Frances and Gloria are "old fashioned," so they provide an opportunity to talk about differences that children experience in different eras. *A Birthday for Frances* also provides an opportunity to talk about different customs surrounding the ways in which birthdays are celebrated in families.

There are several words and phrases that may not be familiar to children because they refer to customs that are no longer practiced or are not practiced in the children's culture. Call out these words and ask children questions that lead them to a deeper understanding of the meaning and a deeper appreciation for the different ways holidays are celebrated.

- ★ Place cards
- ★ Party poppers
- ★ Birthday party customs
  - ■ Cake
  - ■ Candles
  - ■ Singing
  - ■ Blowing out the candles
  - ■ Making a wish

Other Book Recommendations for Social Awareness

Cannon, J. (1993) *Stellaluna*. San Diego: Harcourt Brace.

> A baby bat is separated from her mother and must learn the ways of birds before she is reunited with her mother. In the meantime, she feels lonely, left out, and inadequate.

McGovern, A. (1967). *Too Much Noise*. Boston: Houghton Mifflin.

> Peter becomes annoyed by the noises he hears in his house but quickly learns to appreciate them after following the advice of the village wise man.

Uegaki, C. (2005). *Suki's Kimono*. Tonawanda, NY: Kids Can Press.

> Suki's sisters are embarrassed on the first day of school when Suki wears a kimono given to her by her grandmother. Initially, children tease Suki, but their feelings are quickly transformed into admiration when they listen to Suki describe the festival day when her grandmother bought the kimono for her.

SELF-MANAGEMENT

Strong emotions are a hallmark of early childhood. The intense anticipation of a birthday party or the reaction to a classmate ruining a sand castle can be overwhelming for children. We know that being able to cope with strong emotions is a challenging task for 4- to 6-year-olds (and for many adults!), but that having those skills is important for social and academic success (Denham, 1998; Elias, 2003).

We see it every day. The children who have learned some strategies for coping with the disappointment of a cancelled field trip or the anger of losing a favorite jacket are much better equipped to thrive at school. Some children really need some quiet time when they have strong feelings, but others "shake it out" by closing their eyes, vigorously shaking their hands, and chanting "shake it out, shake it out."

It's important to offer a variety of strategies so children see that these feelings are common and universal and that many people find ways to cope with strong emotions. Having a few strategies in their toolbox helps children see a solution to the feelings that would otherwise be overwhelming and distracting. Strategies need to be taught and practiced initially when children are calm. Gradually, you can coach children to use them in situations that cause strong feelings, and the payoff can be quite noticeable—both in terms of classroom management and academic focus. Recent research is further underscoring the importance of skills like self-regulation for children's school success. As researcher Clancy Blair states, "There is a federal push to learn our numbers, our letters and our words, but a focus on the content, without a focus on the skills required to use that content, will end up with children being left behind" (Nicholson, 2007).

Books where characters model and deal with self-regulation offer a great entry point to begin to teach these skills.

Mean Soup by Betsy Everitt

In *Mean Soup* (1992) by Betsy Everitt, Horace feels really mean at the end of a bad day until he helps his mother make Mean Soup.

Reading 1: Making Sense of the Story

★ Page 6: *What has made it a bad day for Horace?*

★ Page 9: *What does Horace do that tells us he is angry?*

★ Page 12: *What other things does Horace do that tell us he is really angry?*

★ Page 16: *Why does Horace's mom say it is his turn to scream into the pot of soup?*

★ Page 18: *What does it mean to "bare" your teeth? Show me.*

★ Page 20: *Does the soup recipe say to stick out your tongue? Why is Horace's mother sticking out her tongue?*

★ Page 25: *How does Horace feel now? How do you know? Is he still angry?*

Reading 2: Taking It Further

★ Page 3: *Why did it make Horace mad to get a love note from Zelda?*

★ Page 18: *Why does Horace bare his teeth and growl?*

★ Page 22: *What different things does Horace do while he is making mean soup that make him feel better?*

★ Page 23: *Do you think Horace feels like a dragon? Why or why not?*

★ Page 28: *Why is this recipe called Mean Soup?*

★ Page 29: *What does it mean to "stir away a bad day"?*

Reading 3: Making Connections

★ Page 2: *Have you ever forgotten the answer to a question at school? How did you feel?*

★ Page 7: *When you feel mean, what do you do?*

★ Page 18: *If you were making up a recipe for Mean Soup, what would be in it?*

★ Page 23: *Let's pretend we are angry dragons and breathe our best dragon breath.* [Demonstrate with children.] *Now, I don't feel so angry anymore.*

★ Page 29: *Tell us about a time when you had a bad day but you found a way to make it better.*

Classroom Activities to Enhance Self-Management

Soup's On

Bring in a few cookbooks with soup recipes and explain the different parts of a recipe (title, ingredients, cooking steps). Then have each child make his or her own recipe for Mean Soup. Discuss what children do to feel better when they feel mean and angry. Have children draw a picture of themselves making their Mean Soup and let them write or dictate to you the ingredients and steps on the same page. Then compile all the recipes in a class Mean Soup cookbook and keep it in an area of your classroom where children can go to cool off. Consider doing a few variations on Mean Soup such as Excited Omelets or Disappointed Delights.

Cool-Off Corner

It's important for children to have a space that is a retreat when they need a chance to cool off and re-group. Together with your students, choose an area and design and create a space that will be the "cool-off corner" (have them think of their own creative name). Think through all of the elements, such as colors, sounds, furniture, tools (drawing materials, things to squeeze) and make a plan to create this space with the children. Be sure to include some sort of container that holds strategies for calming down: This might be the Mean Soup Cookbook or another resource, such as index cards of individual ideas held in a Treasure Box. Encourage students to visit the cool-off corner when they are feeling overwhelmed like our favorite friends Horace, Alexander, or Lilly.

Vocabulary and Comprehension

Mean Soup ends with the line "And they stood together, stirring away a bad day." The final sentence opens the opportunity to discuss figurative speech. Ask children to show you how to stir away a day. See if they have ideas about what the author means by "stirring away a bad day." If they need help breaking it down, try these questions:

★   *What are the mom and Horace doing together?*

★   *Is it chicken noodle soup or vegetable soup?*

★   *What is special about this soup?*

★   *Does making the soup help Horace feel better?*

★   *Does making it help him "stir the bad day away"?*

Other Book Recommendations for Self-Management

Browne, A. (2006). *Silly Billy.* Cambridge, MA: Candlewick Press.

> To help with his anxiety, Billy uses the worry dolls his grandmother recommends, but he finds that they do not quite solve his problem.

Carr, J. (1995). *Dark Day, Light Night.* New York: Hyperion.

> 'Manda's aunt Ruby helps her deal with some angry feelings by making lists of all the things that they like in the world.

Kroll, S. (1976). *That Makes Me Mad.* New York: Pantheon.

> A little girl gets mad at a lot of things in her daily life but is comforted when she explains her feelings to her mother and her mother understands.

Vail, R. (2002). *Sometimes I'm a Bombaloo.* New York: Scholastic.

> When Katie Honors feels angry and out of control, her mother helps her to be herself again. This book describes the physical signs of anger well, in addition to offering the self-management strategies of giving oneself a time-out to be alone and thinking and finding humor.

RESPONSIBLE DECISION MAKING: ASSUMING PERSONAL RESPONSIBILITY

It might seem a reach to hold young children accountable for responsible decision making, but as with any social skill, decision making can be broken down into teachable and learnable steps that even young children can master. Children begin to learn about making responsible decisions very early in their social interactions with other children. For instance, it is not uncommon for them to argue over the use of a favorite toy. As words are exchanged and feelings get heated, children sometimes strike out and hit or grab the toy. While their short-term goal of getting the toy may be accomplished, they have failed to achieve a much more important goal of interacting with peers in respectful ways. You can help children think through their decisions and the consequences of their decisions.

Responsibility and respect are values that carry meaning throughout one's lifetime, and young children sense the importance of behaving in ways that reflect these values. Consider the following scenario: Several children were involved in an incident where a book on loan from another classroom was damaged. All the children who were involved with the incident denied that they had anything to do with tearing the pages of the book. In spite of the teacher's efforts to talk to the students and understand what happened, no one was willing to explain how the incident happened. Turning to her bibliography, the teacher chose Eve Bunting's *A Day's Work* (1994) to pursue this difficult conversation.

A Day's Work by Eve Bunting

In this book, Francisco, a young Mexican-American boy, tries to help his *abuelo*—his grandfather—find work. Francisco discovers that even though his *abuelo* cannot speak English, he has something even more valuable to teach about telling the truth. (We suggest reading this book four times. Read it the first time without asking questions so children can absorb the whole story before specifically thinking about the different perspectives and feelings of the characters.)

Reading 1: Francisco's Perspective

★　　Page 8: *What does Francisco notice about the man driving the truck?*

How do you think this makes Francisco feel?

Why does Francisco say, "My grandfather is a fine gardener"?

★ Page 18: *What is Francisco thinking about while he works?*

How does Francisco feel when he hears the sounds of splashing and voices from one of the swimming pools nearby?

★ Page 24: *What mistake does Francisco make?*

Why is it hard for Francisco to look at his grandfather?

★ Page 32: *What does Francisco mean when he says he has begun to learn the important things too?*

What did he think was important before? Now what does he understand is important?

Reading 2: Grandfather's Perspective

★ Page 6: *How do you think the grandfather feels when he can't understand English?*

★ Page 20: *How does the grandfather feel when he looks at the brown dirt and the pretty flowers?*

★ Page 24: *What makes Abuelo think he and Francisco have done something wrong if he can't understand the words Ben is saying?*

★ Page 24: *What does the grandfather mean when he says, "We do not lie for work"?*

★ Page 26: *Why is the grandfather sad and not angry?*

What does he mean when he says, "Ask him what we can do?"

What is the price of the lie?

★ Page 30: *What are the important things that the grandfather already knows?*

Reading 3: Making Connections

★ Page 6: *Have you ever been in a situation where you could not understand what was being said?*

How did you feel?

★ Page 12: *Francisco says his grandfather knows about gardening, but that is not true.*

Have you ever said something that was not true. How did you feel?

★ Page 18: *Francisco is working very hard, but he thinks about how proud his mother would be.*

Can you think of a time when you thought about something good to help you get through some hard work? Tell us about it.

★ Page 20: *Francisco and Abuelo are proud of their work. Tell us about a time you felt proud.*

★ Page 24: *Look at each face. How do you think each character is feeling? How do you know?*

★ Page 26: *Francisco feels his heart go weak when his grandfather says they have to fix all the plants.*

How would you feel if you had to fix something that you lied about?

Helping Activities at School

If you have not already done so, identify a number of classroom jobs that can be completed by children that will contribute to the organization, cleanliness, and efficient functioning of the classroom. Some of the traditional classroom jobs include the following:

★ Line leaders

★ Door monitors

★ Lunch helpers

★ Plant caretaker

★ Pet caretaker

★ Attendance checker

★ Library assistant

★ Sweeper

In an effort to stretch your children's social awareness, create additional jobs that focus on noticing and caring for others. These jobs might include the following:

★ Welcome Back Assistant: A weekly job to welcome children who have been absent for one or more days

★ Thank-You Leader: Designate a student to look for opportunities for the class to thank people who have been helpful to them. These might be parent volunteers, a custodian who fixed a broken item in the classroom, a librarian who helped students with a project, or a community person who hosted a field trip. Have thank-you notes on hand to send to that person or have children make personalized thank-you notes.

★ Compassion Champions: Acknowledge children who demonstrate exemplary compassion and caring for others. Highlight how important these behaviors are for the whole class and how each noteworthy act benefits and strengthens the entire class.

Helping Activities at Home

In *A Day's Work*, Francisco has responsibility for translating for his grandfather and for working side by side with him while other children play and frolic in the swimming pool nearby. Francisco is proud of his hard work and the contribution he can make to his family. Children contribute to a family's well being in a number of ways. Ask your students what they do to help their families. Record and tally their responses and review the totals. You can make a graph to show which jobs occur most frequently and which are most unusual. Generate a discussion about how children might be more helpful, which jobs they would like to do, which jobs are fun, which jobs are difficult, and so on. Note the different perspectives on what constitutes fun and difficulty.

Vocabulary and Comprehension

A Day's Work provides rich opportunities for expanding vocabulary and comprehension, beginning with an exposure to Spanish phrases and expressions. The following Spanish words appear in the text:

★ *hace frio*

★ *abuelo*

★ *chorizos*

★ *señora*

★ *gracias*

★ *bueno*

★ *muy bonito*

After you read the words in Spanish, pause and ask the children if they can figure out what the words mean either from the clues in the illustrations or from the context in which the words appear.

The story contains expressions and phrases that may remain obscure to students unless there is some deeper exploration or discussion. Consider calling out the following words using the vocabulary technique described on pages 11–12 and 66–68.

★ omen

★ convinced

★ sloping bank

★ shocked

★ appreciate

★ huddled

In addition, there is a very important phrase towards the end of the story on page 30 that reads, "Words seemed to pass between them, but there were no words." Pause when you read this phrase, then repeat it. Ask the students the following questions:

★ *What does it mean to say "words seemed to pass between them but there were no words"?*

★ *How can you understand another person when there are no words spoken?*

★ *What clues do you look for? Do you see clues in the illustration?*

Havill, J. (1986). *Jamaica's Find*. Boston: Houghton Mifflin.

> Jamaica finds a lost item in the park and struggles with her decision to keep the item and take it home with her.

Heide, F. P. and Gilliland, J. H. (1990). *The Day of Ahmed's Secret*. New York: Scholastic.

> Ahmed has a secret but before he reveals it to his family he fulfills his responsibility of delivering heavy bottles of cooking gas throughout the neighborhood.

Surat, M. (1983). *Angel Child, Dragon Child*. New York: Scholastic.

> Ut, a child from Vietnam, faces taunting and teasing from her classmates because of her language and her clothes. She recognizes her angry response to the teasing and strives to be an angel child rather than a dragon child. Ut and Raymond, when offered the opportunity, figure out a way to resolve the problem.

PROBLEM SOLVING

Children are born problem solvers. From their earliest explorations of their environment, they are sorting, classifying, and adding meaning to their scope of knowledge and trying to make sense of their world. The young toddler who finds a flower blossom on the sidewalk and picks it up and places it back on the bush is exercising her understanding of order and the way things should be.

The rules of social interactions are often much more complex and elusive for children. They cannot push up against the same firm, consistent barriers that they discover in their physical world. Sharing, taking turns, making friends, and waiting may seem like simple tasks; however, feelings can overwhelm children, and they cannot make sense of what they are supposed to do. Therefore, solving problems within a social context can be difficult for them.

With guidance and modeling from adults, even young children can find solutions to their social problems. It can be helpful for children to have experiences in which they approach problem solving in a practical and systematic way. For example, the *Second Step* program (Committee for Children, 2002), a curriculum designed to help children develop social skills, has identified three simple questions to guide young children through a problem-solving process:

★ *How do I feel?*

★ *What is the problem?*

★ *What can I do?*

Once children become familiar with an approach to problem solving, they need opportunities to practice. One form of practice is to coach them through the process in real classroom situations that occur. Another way to offer practice opportunities is to discuss problems that arise in books and apply the process to the situation of the character. For example, in the book *Will I Have a Friend?* by Miriam Cohen (1967), a teacher might ask:

★ *How is Jim feeling?*

★ *What is the problem?*

★ *What can he do?*

Some story situations might never come up in a classroom, and books become a way of introducing thoughtful approaches to problem solving. In other situations, books can be used to prepare children for an anticipated event such as a field trip or welcoming new children to the class.

Enemy Pie by Derek Munson

In the book *Enemy Pie* by Derek Munson (2000), a clever and thoughtful father helps his young child discover that the way to get rid of an enemy is to turn him into a friend.

Reading 1: Child's Perspective

★ Page 1: *Why should this have been a perfect summer?*

★ Page 4: *What is the problem with Jeremy Ross? How does the boy feel?*
  What does it mean to have an enemy?

★ Page 6: *What do you think the dad meant when he says, "enemy pie"?*

★ Page 8: *Why does the boy want to put disgusting things into the pie?*
  How does the boy feel about the pie?

★ Page 14: *The father bakes the pie. What is the boy's job?*

★ Pages 17–18: *What are some of the things that the boy and Jeremy Ross do together?*

★ Page 23: *What happens when the boys are in the tree house?*

★ Page 28: *Why does the boy say, "Jeremy, don't eat it!"?*

★ Page 31: *How does the boy lose his best enemy?*

Reading 2: Other Characters' Perspectives

★ Page 6: *Why does the father tell the boy that he had enemies when he was the same age?*

★ Page 15: *Why is Jeremy surprised when he answers the door?*

★ Page 24: *Why does the boy let Jeremy into his tree house?*

★ Page 26: *Look at this picture. What would you say about how the boys feel? How do you know?*

★ Page 31: *What is the secret the dad keeps about enemy pie?*

Reading 3: Making Connections

★ Page 4: *How would you feel if someone laughed at you and left you out?*

★ Page 6: *The boy's father suggests making an enemy pie. What would you do if you had an enemy?*

★ Page 10: *The boy plays by himself by tossing a basketball and throwing a boomerang. What do you do when you play alone?*

★ Page 14: *What does the boy mean when he says, "It was worth a try"?*

★ Page 22: *Do you have a place you like to go that is just your own, like the boy's tree house? Tell us about it.*

★ Page 30: *Why is the enemy pie delicious?*

★ Page 31: *What is the secret ingredient of enemy pie? Or what is "magic" about enemy pie?*

Classroom Activities to Enhance Problem Solving

Make Lemonade

The story of *Enemy Pie* is about taking something bad and turning it into something good. In the Make Lemonade game, children are given the opportunity to practice looking for positive aspects of a situation that might appear unpleasant or bad from their perspective. Ask students what is meant by the expression, "When life gives you lemons, make lemonade." If necessary, explain to students that lemons represent something unpleasant or disappointing, just like the taste of unsweetened lemon juice. If you are able to take a disappointment or an unpleasant experience and turn it into something positive, it would be like making sweet lemonade out of sour lemons.

For each situation, ask your students to think of someone or something for which the event might be beneficial. Read the situation and then ask, "Who can make lemonade?"

★ You planned on going to a Fourth of July picnic with your cousins. It is pouring rain, and the picnic is cancelled.

★ You chose your favorite sweater to wear to school and discovered that it was too small for you.

★ You worked very hard to save money to buy a special card for your grandmother. When you delivered the card to her house, you see the same card on her coffee table. Your cousin has given her the same one.

More Than One Way

A key to successful problem solving is the ability to see multiple solutions to a problem. In this activity, children practice generating ideas to solve a typical problem. The purpose of the exercise is to give children the opportunity to learn that there is often more than one way to solve a problem and that the ideas and contributions of others can often lead to a successful solution.

Read each of the scenarios below, or make up situations based on the experiences of the children in your class, and ask your students to generate ideas for solutions. Encourage creative—even absurd—but workable solutions. Record all suggestions but agree beforehand that none of the solutions can consist of actions that could hurt anyone. At the end of the brainstorming, summarize the solutions and highlight how many possible ways there are to solve problems.

★ Liam enjoys the after-school programs he attends three days a week while his mother is at work. His best friend, Henry, does not attend the program, so Liam only sees him during the school day. Jordan, a new friend from the after-school program, has started joining Liam and Henry at recess, and Henry is jealous. Jordan asks Liam if just the two of them could play together at recess since they only get to play with each other after school. Liam is confused. He likes Jordan and doesn't want to leave him out at recess, but Henry is his best friend and has asked just to play with him. What can Liam do?

★ Trunell and Sabika have been collecting colorful elastic wristbands together. They have asked all the members of their families to be on the lookout for the stretchy bracelets; Sabika's mother has just found a large collection of over 100 wristbands at her work and has offered them to Sabika. Sabika is very excited to add these to the collection, but she remembers that she and Trunell have agreed to share all the bracelets they find. Now Sabika is unsure. She would like to keep this large collection of wristbands her mother has given her. What should Sabika do?

★ Sten and his cousin Bert have played soccer together since they were five. They both tried out for the neighborhood soccer team. Bert was asked to join, but Sten was not. Bert was very excited to make the team until he saw Sten's sad face. What can Bert say to Sten?

Vocabulary and Comprehension

One of the reasons the boy in *Enemy Pie* had a difficult time with his "enemy" is that he expected and wanted his summer to be perfect. The appearance of Jeremy did not fit the boy's expectation of what constituted a perfect summer. By encouraging your students to broaden the scope of what is satisfying to them and to reframe a situation, you will be helping them understand an important dimension of problem solving. Begin with a discussion of perfect.

★ *What does it mean to be perfect?*

★ *What is a good thing about a "perfect" situation/thing/person?*

★ *What is NOT so good about a "perfect" situation/thing/person?*

★ *Can someone be perfect all the time?*

The main character in *Enemy Pie* is jealous and hurt because his best friend, Stanley, is invited to Jeremy's party, and he is not. His jealousy takes over his ability to think about the situation, and he focuses on all of Jeremy's bad qualities. Ask your students to think about how the story might have been different if the boy had talked himself through the following situation taking a different perspective:

"I sure didn't like it when Jeremy smiled when he struck me out in the baseball game. But maybe it wasn't a mean smile. Maybe it was a smile about feeling good about himself in a game with a bunch of new kids. I hadn't thought about that."

"It was no fun to be left out of a birthday party, but maybe I seemed unfriendly at the baseball game, and Jeremy didn't think I liked him. I guess he invited Stanley because he knows him and he lives right next door. Hmm. Maybe I had something to do with this situation."

Other Book Recommendations for Problem Solving

Fox, M. (1985). *Wilfrid Gordon McDonald Partridge*. Brooklyn: Kane/Miller.

A young boy learns to understand what memory is and then helps his friend find her memory in a sensitive and creative way.

Henkes, K. (1996). *Lilly's Purple Plastic Purse*. New York: HarperCollins.

Lilly loves everything about school especially her teacher, but when he asks her to wait a while before showing her new purse, she does something she later regrets.

Rosa-Casanova, S. (1997). *Mama Provi and the Pot of Rice*. New York: Simon & Schuster.

When her granddaughter becomes ill, Mama Provi decides to make her a pot of chicken and rice, but Mama Provi only knows how to cook meals for dozens of people. She solves her problem with the help of her friendly neighbors.

DIALOGIC READING'S FLEXIBILITY IN YOUR CLASSROOM

You may encounter parents who question the use of dialogic reading in your classroom. In talking to parents, we suggest that you focus the conversation on best practices as you listen to their concerns. Review the research that tells us that young children's development is exploding across multiple domains and teaching across those domains is the best way to maximize impact (Blair, 2002). For example, if you incorporate movement in a basic mathematics activity, that addition creates a synergy that furthers development. If you take an emergent literacy activity, like dialogic reading, and add a social-emotional element, the overlap between the two areas creates a more powerful instructional "punch." Skill development in emergent literacy supports social-emotional growth that in turn reinforces emergent literacy gains. The parent may not understand the value of social-emotional issues, but in reality, adding that dimension to the lesson is a sophisticated instructional decision.

Social-emotional learning and emergent literacy are natural partners; they both rely on language for success. You might explain to parents how you had taken *A Day's Work*, a beautiful book about a child's dilemma, and used it to develop children's social-emotional skills such as empathy and responsible decision making. Share that while addressing those areas that are critical for school success, you were also developing emergent literacy skills such as vocabulary, comprehension, and expressive and receptive language; however, you were focusing on those areas with a social-emotional "twist." This added layer made the instruction richer than a more traditional emergent literacy lesson. Encourage parents to come observe and possibly to even learn about dialogic reading and volunteer to lead a reading group. Urge them to look for growth in their child's language skills and social-emotional competence and then check back in a month to see if the parents still have concerns.

CHAPTER 3

LANGUAGE AND LITERACY SKILLS

Comprehension, vocabulary, and narrative structure are some of the building blocks of language and literacy. The three elements work together to strengthen a child's experience with stories and language. Dialogic reading is a flexible tool to help you add a layer of intentionality and richness to children's language development.

One of dialogic reading's well-studied benefits is children's growth in receptive and expressive language. (See Figure 1.4: Research on Dialogic Reading, page 31.) This outcome seems logical given the intense focus on conversations during the repeated readings in small groups. Other aspects of language such as comprehension and vocabulary are also logical companions to dialogic reading. Narrative structure is a critical piece of comprehension that complements dialogic reading as well. By putting these pieces together, the dialogic reading experience continues to deepen for you and your students.

COMPREHENSION

Young children's natural sense of curiosity drives them to make meaning of the world around them. They are trying to make sense of what they see, hear, touch, and taste, and stories are just one piece of the giant puzzle around them. Why does it rain? Why does Ferdinand smell the flowers? Why can't I see a dinosaur?

Comprehension is a vital piece of early literacy instruction (Applebee, Langer, & Mullis, 1988; Morrow, 1997). Young children are capable of complex and sophisticated thinking, but comprehension itself is a complicated concept. Understanding an event in a story might involve knowing the vocabulary used. Ramona brings this to light in a humorous way for readers of *Ramona the Pest* when she is wondering about "the dawnzer lee light" in the "puzzling song" that Miss Binney teaches them (Cleary, 1968). It is the first day of kindergarten, and Ramona is finding many things confusing. Miss Binney is teaching them the national anthem, of course, and Ramona reminds us how what children hear is not always what we intend. The teacher is saying "dawn's early light" which makes perfect sense to her, but to Ramona it is "dawnzer lee light," which she determines must be another word for a lamp. Ramona is not too far off, but a little explanation from the teacher would have aided comprehension. During the give and take of dialogic reading, you can realize the comprehension errors that children make, e.g. "dawnzer lee light," and help them discover the author's meaning.

Comprehension sometimes involves having familiarity with the context, which could include some background knowledge. For example, *Amazing Grace* (Hoffman, 1991) is full of allusions to events in history and literature. Grace enjoys acting out battles as if she were Joan of Arc, weaving webs like Anansi the Spider, hiding in a wooden horse at the gates of Troy, being Hiawatha sitting by the shining Big-Sea-Water, acting like Mowgli in the jungle, or rubbing a magic lamp like Aladdin. The illustrations may help children understand the basic idea of these scenarios, but they are much richer if they know the stories behind Joan of Arc's bravery or the trick of the Trojan Horse. In short, comprehension is deepened by having more background knowledge. You can tailor the background knowledge you address to the needs of the group. For some small groups, the story of the Trojan Horse is beyond their reach and thus would be irrelevant. Others are perfectly ready to dive into the story of Joan of Arc and will find it fascinating. Working with small groups gives you this flexibility.

Making sense of the passage of time and the sequence of story events can fill in important pieces of understanding for children. For example, in *Noisy Nora* (Wells, 1973), a girl grows weary of being ignored by her parents who are attending to her siblings. Nora finally decides to run away, and her family becomes worried and begins searching for her. At the end of the story, she comes bursting out of the closet, and the family is overjoyed. The relief of Nora's family when she reappears is lost on a child who does not realize that time has passed, and Nora has actually been missing for a while. This understanding of time is an important piece of the overall comprehension of the story.

Comprehension is an umbrella under which many skills gather. Attending to the individual skills and the larger concept will prepare children well for later formal literacy instruction.

ENCOURAGING COMPREHENSION

★ Dialogic reading gives teachers a structure in which to ask meaningful questions to help children comprehend the story.

- We know that children are capable of responding to the complexities of text when they are prompted with meaningful questions (McKeown & Beck, 2003). Asking questions that probe beyond recalling language from the text or from you takes practice and intentionality.

- Dialogic reading develops the habit of questioning and an awareness of language from you and your students. These habits alone will help aid students' comprehension.

- Questions that focus on the social-emotional elements of a story often probe at some of the complexities of a story. For example, in *Lilly's Purple Plastic Purse* (Henkes, 1996), Lilly feels conflicted about the situation with her teacher. She adores Mr. Slinger, but she is angry and embarrassed when he takes away her purse because she can't stop playing with it during class. Those layers of emotions take some unpacking to really comprehend. Questioning Lilly's feelings helps children do the unpacking and build understanding.

★ Scaffold children's understanding. As you encourage children to stretch their vocabularies and comprehension skills, add the support they need. Pause after a complicated passage and help children unpack it. (Refer to *Fish is Fish* example in Chapter 1, pages 11–12.) Then read the passage again before you move on.

- Model your own thinking aloud. If you encounter an unusual illustration, make your thinking explicit by narrating your own thought process. For example, while reading *Gingerbread Baby* (Brett, 1999), you might say, "This is an unusual picture. There is one big picture and a smaller picture on each side. What is going on in this small picture? What is the boy doing? I see that there is a gingerbread shape around the picture. I see that Matti is mixing up the dough and rolling it out. Where is Matti?" Brett uses this device of placing smaller pictures of different scenes occurring simultaneously on either side of the main scene. By figuring out aloud how the picture works, you will help children understand how to approach confusing illustrations in other books.

★ Make predictions. During the first reading of a book, pause and examine the cover with students. Ask what they see and what they think the book might be about. At important moments in the plot, pause and ask children what they think will happen next. Push them to explain why they think that will occur.

- The emotions of characters often drive the plot. Use these opportunities to ask about how characters are feeling and why. Encourage students to connect how emotions relate to what will happen next in the story.

★ At the end of a reading, summarize the story. As children become familiar with this practice, have them begin to do the summarizing. Consider using a few cards from key points in the story (see the Narrative Structure section, page 69) or flipping back to the relevant pages.

★ Have props available for children to do literacy-related dramatic play. Also have children use them for retelling familiar stories. For example, for the story *The Mitten* by Alvin Tresselt (1964), provide a large blanket under which children can hide as they seek shelter from the cold. They can act out the characters as they approach the mitten: "Is there room for me in that nice warm mitten?" The children under the blanket provide the chorus and help the little mouse each time a new character approaches and asks for shelter: "Not much space left but come in. We'll see what we can do."

★ Make connections anywhere you can. Choose books that you will be able to relate to something children recently learned or experienced. Knowledge builds on knowledge. For example, after taking your class to the local civic parade, read *Curious George at the Parade* (Rey & Rey, 1999) and talk about similarities and differences between the real and fictional parades.

★ Build vocabulary knowledge intentionally. Vocabulary obviously plays a tremendous role in comprehension. Building vocabulary while also incorporating these other comprehension strategies gives children a meaningful experience with a story. The added layers of intentionality fill in the gaps and scaffold their understanding.

VOCABULARY

Teachers and parents have intuitively recognized that young children are fascinated by new, complex, and lyrical words. A generation of children grew up singing "Supercalifragilisticexpialidocious" or precociously repeating "antidisestablishmentarianism." And the chanting of young children has filled classrooms with the repeated name refrain of "Tikki tikki tembo-no sa rembo-chari bari ruchi-pip peri pembo" (Mosel, 1968). But the importance of vocabulary development for student success extends beyond the exotic and unusual combinations of sounds.

Research is beginning to catch up with intuition in discerning the ways in which young children develop vocabulary and the importance of vocabulary development to later success. There is a strong and established relationship between students' vocabulary knowledge and their ability to successfully comprehend what they read. The startling findings of Hart and Risley in their keystone work *Meaningful Differences in the Everyday Experience of Young Children* (1995) calls attention to the magnitude of differences in vocabulary acquisition in American families. Over a period of two and a half years, researchers recorded for one hour each month every word spoken at home between parent and child. There were startling differences between families in how much interaction and talking typically went on in the home.

Those children who were raised in homes with the highest frequency of verbal interaction would hear 11 million words in a year compared to children in homes with the least frequency of verbal interaction who would hear only 3 million words. This large difference to early exposure to language is linked to large differences in child outcomes at age 9. The data from the study highlights the importance of early language development and particularly the need for adults to talk to children in meaningful ways that help them extend their understanding of language.

In an important study about vocabulary acquisition, Warwick Elley found that children acquired new vocabulary from listening to stories read three times in a week. The results were even more robust when the teacher added explanations about unfamiliar words and when the word appeared within a familiar context (Elley, 1989). Vocabulary development occurs through repeated exposure to words, conversations, and incidental learning from verbal contexts as well as through direct instruction. With its focus on repeated reading and its question-generated conversations about the story, dialogic reading provides a natural yet systematic method for you to increase student language, and in particular, student vocabulary.

GETTING STARTED WITH A VOCABULARY STRATEGY

Dialogic reading's hallmark of guided conversations occurring in repeated readings in small groups offers a helpful context within which powerful vocabulary learning can occur. Selecting appropriate stories and then selecting appropriate words within the stories to highlight during the readings becomes the first step in helping students increase vocabulary and deepen comprehension. It is very important to provide a variety of reading material that will appeal to the wide range of student interests and learning styles. More specifically, when selecting stories for children to hear in the small groups, don't be afraid to stretch the children beyond their current level. Gradually increase the length of the books that you read. Consider introducing chapter books that require students to prolong the completion of a story and to retain story lines over time. In addition, there is increasing evidence about the importance of reading nonfiction books to children. Generally, this genre of book does not have the same appeal to teachers as storybooks, but children need exposure to factual information, particularly about science. Nonfiction books work best with young children if the books are introduced in response to expressed interest or curiosity on the part of the children. If a bird's nest is found in the tree adjacent to the playground and the children ask questions, this is the perfect opportunity to bring in books about different kinds of birds, habitats, and nests. Provide books for reference that children can easily look through after you have read the books aloud and guided them through the information.

It might be tempting to look for the most unusual or obscure words in a story to highlight for vocabulary development, but that may not be the most important criteria to consider. Authors may choose words for their sounds, rhythm, or alliteration to the rest of the sentence, but the key words to choose for vocabulary development are the ones that are instrumental to understanding the story. There are many interesting words such as *jaunty, encyclopedias,* and *lurched* in Kevin Henkes book *Lilly's Purple Plastic Purse* (1996), but children do not need to know the meaning of these words to understand the story. However, if children do not understand the words *considerate* and *longed for*, they will miss a key part of Lilly's emotional response and reaction to Mr. Slinger's taking her purse and glasses away from her. These are the key words you should call out for vocabulary development.

In an example from *Ramona the Pest* the issue is not the complexity or subtlety of the word *present*, but the fact that the word has more than one meaning. Ramona is visiting her kindergarten class for the very first time. The teacher leads her to the little tables and chairs and says, "Sit here for the present." Ramona is thrilled. She imagines what kind of present the teacher will give her. She notices that not all of the children are told about the present, and so she feels particularly special. She waits patiently even though waiting is hard. Eventually the teacher realizes Ramona's misunderstanding and that she should have used a different word.

This example leads to the next step in a strategy for vocabulary development: choosing a word that has the same or similar meaning and repeating the sentence using that different word. Miss Binney explains to Ramona that when she used the word *present*, she meant "for now:" "I meant that I wanted you to sit here for now, because later I may have the children sit at different desks." Although puzzled by the fact that the same word could mean different things, Ramona immediately understood what Ms. Binney really meant. You can elaborate and expand on the sentence to ensure an even more secure understanding.

Ideally, once you have rephrased the sentence and given contextual cues, you can engage children in a conversation about the word and its meaning. In the case of Ramona, you have an opportunity to talk about language and misunderstandings in other situations. For example you might say, "I can understand why Ramona was confused by the word *present*. Usually when we hear the word *present*, we think about a gift, but this story lets us know that we need to pay attention to more than just words. Who can think of another word that means more than one thing?" (bark, light, to/too/two) This type of exercise can alert children to look for cues beyond the sound of the word and to develop skills for discerning meaning and understanding.

A final step in teaching vocabulary is to repeat the original sentence with the unfamiliar word. Hearing the sentence again, after students have background information on the meaning of the words, will increase the likelihood that they will recognize the word the next time they hear it. If you focus on a particular vocabulary word in Reading 1 or 2, be sure to pause and check for understanding on subsequent readings.

CHAPTER 3: Language and Literacy Skills

1. **Select appropriate and relevant stories or nonfiction books related to students' interests.**
2. **Identify vocabulary words in the story that are key to comprehension.**
3. **Repeat the sentence using a word that has the same or similar meaning.**
4. **Engage students in a dialogue about the word, its context, and its meaning.**
5. **Repeat the sentence using the original, unfamiliar word.**

ENCOURAGING VOCABULARY DEVELOPMENT

★ *New words bulletin board:* Designate a part of your classroom bulletin board surface as a place where you can post new words that you discuss during your readings or during conversations. Refer to the new words from time to time and develop ways of alerting your students to how they might use the words in context.

★ *Play the Say It a Different Way game:* Challenge your students to use more complex words or to use the words that you have discussed as vocabulary words. Model the ways that they can say the same things using different words: "The clouds were big. The clouds were huge. The clouds were enormous."

★ *Increase conversation:* Keeping in mind the findings of Hart and Risley (1995), pay attention to the ways in which you can increase conversation in your classroom. Choose topics to discuss during snack or lunch time that will engage children. Encourage them to elaborate if they start with short, simple statements:

Child: *I went to my cousin's.*

Teacher: *So, you went to your cousin's house this weekend. Did you stay all night? Who went with you?*

★ *Choose books with challenging words:* We may be underestimating children's capacity to listen to and learn from complex books and stories. In stories like *Stellaluna* (Cannon, 1993), the author does not hold back from using complicated words and sophisticated references. Talk with your children about the words and ask them if they can figure out what the words mean. Use the flexibility of dialogic reading's small groups to choose vocabulary words that are relevant to that specific group's needs. Needs may vary from group to group.

NARRATIVE STRUCTURE

An important part of reading comprehension is grasping the basic plot or the unfolding of events in the story. To sequence events in a story, children must understand cause and effect. For example, in the popular fairy tale of the three little pigs, the sequence of events can be described in the following way:

Wolf is hungry.

Wolf looks for pigs.

Wolf destroys pigs' houses of straw and sticks.

Pigs worry about how to protect themselves from wolf.

Pigs build house of bricks.

Wolf can't blow house down.

Wolf discovers chimney.

Pigs boil water and capture wolf.

The components of the plot must proceed in this order for the story to make sense. Each event causes the next. Try taking the above events and rearranging them. The story no longer makes sense.

Reading children's books offers an easy opportunity to talk more about cause-and-effect and, specifically, narrative structure—the fact that stories have a beginning, middle, and end. When you are asking children to figure out a story's beginning, middle, and end, you are engaging them in a cause-and-effect exercise.

The process of breaking down a story into these components helps children comprehend the story better. This skill is also useful in other areas such as planning. Planning to make lunch involves breaking down a complex idea into its parts and sequencing them. You don't wash your hands at the end nor do you start by putting the pieces of bread together. Similarly, social-emotional skills follow a sequence. To solve a problem, you start by identifying the problem not with brainstorming solutions. These sound like simple concepts, but for young children, such a task is incredibly complicated and must be simplified.

Sequencing also helps children follow directions. If you say to children, "Get ready to go home," the task can be overwhelming. However, with some sequencing skills, children can begin to ask, "What do I do first? What do I do next? What is the last thing I do before going home?" It might even help children to think of the task by location: "Start with the hook by the book nook and get your coat and backpack; then move to your desk and load your backpack with your take-home packet; finally line up at the door."

ENCOURAGING AN UNDERSTANDING OF NARRATIVE STRUCTURE

★ One piece of understanding narrative structure is knowing the basic vocabulary. Teach students the words that signal sequencing, such as *first, next, then, before, after, when,* and *finally.* Use and emphasize these words frequently in songs, signs, and everyday conversation. Many teachers are enhancing their students' learning by using sign language in their classrooms. To help visual and kinesthetic learners, teach the signs for these sequencing words and incorporate those as well.

  ■ Give children information on the sequence of events that will occur in their day. Provide the information verbally as well as with a class schedule posted on the wall. Refer to the schedule regularly, and use the sequencing words in your description. Provide pictures paired with the activity words.

★ All stories incorporate some element of sequence in their beginning, middle, and end of the story. Use the opportunity at the end of a reading to have children discuss the beginning, middle, and end. Provide props to encourage them to act out familiar stories. For example, provide two tin pails and some blueberries so that children can enjoy hearing the "kuplink, kuplank, kuplunk" sounds as they act out *Blueberries for Sal* (McCloskey, 1948). As children retell, they are sequencing the events. You could even provide a jar for the canning of the jam at the end so the props almost serve as bookends marking the story's beginning and end.

  ■ Dialogic reading's repeated readings help children develop an understanding of narrative structure. The familiarity of the story makes retelling easier. At the end of your final reading, do a sequencing activity with three story cards made from pages of three significant events in the narrative.[3] After the final reading, ask children to put the cards in order of the story's events and then use the pictures to retell the story in their own words.

  Some stories lend themselves easily to more in-depth, cross-curricular sequencing activities.

  ■ *The Very Hungry Caterpillar* by Eric Carle (1969) follows a caterpillar from egg to butterfly. The sequence is a great example of concrete, dramatic change that has to occur in the appropriate order for it to make sense.

    1. A little egg lies on a leaf.

    2. The tiny caterpillar emerges from the egg.

    3. A tiny caterpillar eats and grows.

    4. A chrysalis forms around the caterpillar.

    5. It turns into a beautiful butterfly.

---

[3] Copyright law allows you to make one copy of no more than two pages from a children's book. So choose the two most significant chronological events in the story and photocopy those pages. Then draw a picture of the third significant chronological event.

Teachers can find photographs or drawings of this life cycle (or use *The Very Hungry Caterpillar* story cards that are available commercially) and ask children to put them in the correct order. It's important to put them in an incorrect order first and then discuss why that sequence would not be possible. This demonstrates understanding of cause and effect—a crucial aspect of sequencing.

★ Sequencing occurs all around us. Take advantage of easy, fun opportunities to point it out.

- ■ Have children cut out pictures in magazines of people at different ages—from babies to grandparents. Together, put the pictures in the correct growth sequence and talk about what toddlers can do that babies cannot, what your students can do that toddlers cannot, and so on. Use as many sequencing words as possible—for example, *after, before, next, then, finally,* and *initially.*

- ■ Make simple cards (draw them or cut out pictures) showing the steps of routine activities that children know, such as making a sandwich. Have them put the cards in the appropriate order and describe how to do the activity. For a greater challenge, give children blank cards and markers and have them draw their own pictures of the sequence of getting ready for school or bed. Then have them put the cards in the correct order and tell you about it. Swap the positions of two cards and ask a child if that change matters. Have her explain why.

★ Simply talking through experiences (yours or your students') models the language of sequence.

- ■ A way to add some complexity and fun to sharing stories is to take turns telling about the day's highs and lows. This is best done with a small group—perhaps during lunch, snack, or as a small-group activity. At first, you should be the one to call on the others to talk. Before you begin, think of a pattern for the sequence of who talks; for example, you might choose oldest to youngest or shortest to tallest. Once everyone has shared, the group tries to figure out the pattern you used to call on people. For example, was it alphabetical order by first name? Children are having fun as they problem solve about sequences (Merryman, 2007). This is a great activity to share with families, who can use it at the dinner table.

CONCLUSION: THE POWER OF REPEATED READING WITH SMALL-GROUP INSTRUCTION

Wise school administrators and policy makers recognize that the most powerful classroom tool is the teacher. The variables that seem most important to optimal student outcomes might possibly be how passionate you feel about teaching, how supported you feel in your efforts, and how connected you feel to your students and their families. Improved test scores, love of learning, and social competence are benefits that fall into place if teachers find their own voices in teaching lessons in their classrooms and are able to provide intentional and thoughtful experiences for students.

New ideas, techniques, and strategies provide ways for you to keep the teaching experience dynamic and stimulating. The tips and examples that are covered in this book derive from the real classroom experiences of teachers. Many of you may already be reading stories, working in small groups, and attending to the social and emotional development of your students. By raising your awareness of the research behind dialogic reading and providing you with a range of strategies, we hope that you will feel inspired to review your classroom practice so that it is more efficient, more enjoyable, and more interesting for both you and your students.

How to Become Familiar With Dialogic Reading

The Power of Repeated Reading in Small-Group Instruction © 2008 by Wendie Bramwell & Brooke Graham Doyle • Scholastic Professional

Select a favorite children's book and reread it. A short book works best.

★ Read the book three times with small groups to become familiar with dialogic reading.

★ Ask only a few questions during each reading to become comfortable with the types of questions and the rhythm of stopping to engage in dialogue while also managing a small group.

★ You'll also be practicing the different types of responses—validating, expanding, repeating, and correcting—to children's answers.

Reading 1 Practice

The goal of the first reading is to get familiar with the book. Discussing any unfamiliar vocabulary words is important during this reading.

★ During the first reading, pause three or four times to ask questions such as these:

What is _____ [character in the story] doing?

Why does _____ [event from story] happen?

★ Focus on repeating children's answers during this reading practice. See the example below for *A Pocket for Corduroy* (Freeman, 1978):

Teacher: *What does Corduroy want?*

Child: *A pocket.*

Teacher: *A pocket.*

Reading 2 Practice

The goal of the second reading is to deepen comprehension.

★ During the second reading, pause three or four times and ask questions such as these:

How does _____ [character) feel? Why?

What is happening on this page?

★ Focus on expanding children's answers during this reading practice.

Teacher: *What is Corduroy looking for?*

Child: *A pocket.*

Teacher: *Corduroy is looking for something to make a pocket. He notices he doesn't have a pocket.*

1

The Power of Repeated Reading in Small-Group Instruction © 2008 by Wendie Bramwell & Brooke Graham Doyle • Scholastic Professional

Reading 3 Practice

The goal of the third reading is to have children become storytellers and to connect the book to their own experiences.

★ During the third reading, pause three or four times and ask questions such as these:

What happens next?

Has this ever happened to you?

★ Focus on affirming children when they answer—with facial expressions, body language, and/or words.

Teacher: *Have you ever lost something that was special to you?*

Child: *I lost my special blanket. It was yellow and fuzzy with green frogs on it.*

Teacher: [nodding, with sympathetic facial expression] *Losing your blanket must have made you sad.*

2

How to Develop a Set of Dialogic Reading Questions

The Power of Repeated Reading in Small-Group Instruction © 2008 by Wendie Bramwell & Brooke Graham Doyle • Scholastic Professional

After becoming familiar with the basic rhythm of dialogic reading and practicing with some generic questions, you're ready to develop your own set of questions for the three readings of a book.

★ Pick a book you know your children will enjoy.

★ For each reading, you will develop about six to eight questions.

  ■ Think about the goal of each reading and how your questions will change over the three readings.

  ■ Decide how to space the questions so that the pacing of questions versus reading feels comfortable for you.

★ Use the template on page 3 to develop your questions. Page 2 provides a sample using the classic, *A Pocket for Corduroy* (Freeman, 1978).

1

Set of Dialogic Reading Questions for *A Pocket for Corduroy*

(Note: Many children's books do not list page numbers. For those books, we calculate page numbers by counting the first page of the story's text as page 1.)

READING 1	READING 2	READING 3
Goal: Familiarize children with the book; discuss critical vocabulary.	Goal: Deepen children's comprehension.	Goal: Children become storytellers; they connect the book to their experiences.
Page 7: What does Corduroy want?	Page 8: Why doesn't Corduroy want to use the towel or washcloths for his pocket?	Page 7: What happens next?
Page 10: Why does Corduroy crawl into the laundry bag?	Page 11: Why does Lisa leave Corduroy in the Laundromat?	Page 10: Where have you always wanted to live?
Page 15: What thoughtful thing does the artist do for Corduroy?	Page 12: How do you think Lisa feels about leaving Corduroy at the Laundromat?	Page 14: What is happening on this page?
Page 22: How does Corduroy feel when he ends up in the empty laundry basket? Why?	Page 17: What does the manager say when it's time for the Laundromat to close?	Page 16: What kind of painting would you draw if you saw that?
Page 26: How does Lisa feel when she finds Corduroy? How do you know?	Page 19: How is the soap like snow?	Page 19: What happens next?
Page 28: Why does Lisa put a card in Corduroy's pocket?	Page 27: What does Lisa do that lets Corduroy know she is happy to find him?	Page 28: How does Corduroy feel? How does Lisa feel? How do you know?

The Power of Repeated Reading in Small-Group Instruction © 2008 by Wendie Bramwell & Brooke Graham Doyle • Scholastic Professional

2

Template for a Set of Dialogic Readings

The Power of Repeated Reading in Small-Group Instruction © 2008 by Wendie Bramwell & Brooke Graham Doyle • Scholastic Professional

READING 1 Goal: Familiarize children with the book; discuss critical vocabulary.	READING 2 Goal: Deepen children's comprehension.	READING 3 Goal: Children become storytellers; they connect the book to their experiences.

3

HANDOUT 2: How to Develop a Set of Dialogic Reading Questions

Important Points for Families to Know About Repeated Reading

The Power of Repeated Reading in Small-Group Instruction © 2008 by Wendie Bramwell & Brooke Graham Doyle • Scholastic Professional

Children are great listeners. They can pick up words, tone of voice, and often express whole sentences at surprising moments. You can help your child do well in school by doing the most simple thing—talk to him or her! If you need help starting a conversation with your child, read a book to your child using a questioning technique. Often the questions will open up a topic, and before you know it, you and your child will be taking turns, listening, talking, and questioning.

Here are some questions to help you get started with any book you choose:

★ *What is happening on this page?*

★ *Has this ever happened to you?*

★ *Why did* _____ [fill in with a detail from the story]*?*

★ *What do you notice in the illustrations?* [point to specific parts of the illustrations]

★ *What happens next?*

★ *How does* _____ [character's name] *feel?*

★ *When have you felt this way?*

★ Use what you know about your child's experiences that relate to the characters in the book.

★ After your child answers a question, respond by repeating and/or expanding the answer.

Enjoy talking with your child!

TEACHER REFLECTION SHEET 1:
Language—What Do I Say?

The Power of Repeated Reading in Small-Group Instruction © 2008 by Wendie Bramwell & Brooke Graham Doyle • Scholastic Professional

Many teachers are unaware of the preponderance of questions they pose to children that require either a yes/no or a one-word response. With increasing evidence that children's language development in the early years is related to later school success, you need strategies for optimally using your own language as a model and stimulation for children's language development.

Use the following suggestion to raise awareness of the language used in the classroom and help develop strategies for changing some of the habitual questions that limit the practice of language for children.

Tape record a typical lesson or activity such as arrival, departure, or morning circle time. Listen to the tape and transcribe the questions you ask on the form on page 3. For each question that requires only a one-word or a yes/no response, rewrite it in such a way so children will have to say more. See the example on page 2.

1

TEACHER REFLECTION Sheet 1

Original Questions	Improved Questions
Do you have everything you need?	How do I know if you are ready to go home?
How was your bus ride today?	What was the best part of the bus ride?
Has anyone seen the key to the bike shed?	I've looked on the hook and on the shelf and I can't find the key to the bike shed. Do you have any ideas about where it might be?
Did you like this book?	What happened in this book?
It's a beautiful picture, isn't it?	What makes this such a beautiful picture?

The Power of Repeated Reading in Small-Group Instruction © 2008 by Wendie Bramwell & Brooke Graham Doyle • Scholastic Professional

2

Asking for More

Use this form to record questions you ask during class. As necessary, rewrite the questions in such a way that children are required to use more language when they answer.

Original Questions	Improved Questions

3

The Power of Repeated Reading in Small-Group Instruction © 2008 by Wendie Bramwell & Brooke Graham Doyle • Scholastic Professional

TEACHER REFLECTION Sheet 1

TEACHER REFLECTION SHEET 2: Affirmations

The purpose of this reflection is to increase your awareness of how you use language with young children. Noticing your own habits will allow you the opportunity to make a change. Sometimes the smallest change will freshen up the way children experience language.

Check In

1. Take ten minutes to tape record yourself during a time of day when you are interacting with the children. This might be when children arrive, when they are preparing to leave for the day, or perhaps during a group time. Listen to the recording and tally the number of times you do the following:

    ∽ How many times did I say, "Good job!"? _____

    ∽ How many times did I use a child's name? _____

    ∽ How many times did I repeat the same instructions? _____

    ∽ How many times did I use a specific affirmation (one that fit the situation precisely)? _____

    ∽ What words did I say more than five times? _____

2. Review the results of your survey and determine where you would like to make changes.

    Change Suggestions:

    If you would like to decrease the number of times you say, "Good job":

    ∽ Engage the children in this exercise: Create a Good Job jar by filling a jar with tokens. Have children listen for when you say "Good job." When they hear it, they can remove a token from the Good Job jar. The goal is to keep all of the tokens in the jar. Chart your improvement over time together with children. Explain that you are trying to use more interesting words than "Good job."

The Power of Repeated Reading in Small-Group Instruction © 2008 by Wendie Bramwell & Brooke Graham Doyle • Scholastic Professional

1

If you would like to increase the use of children's names:

∿ Each day, write the names of three children on a sticky note and place it where you will

see it throughout the day. Make a point of saying something specifically to these three children.

Select three different children each day.

If you would like to reduce the number of times you give instructions to children:

∿ Think about how you can prepare children to hear instructions clearly the first time you

deliver them. Ensure that you have their attention, and don't say anything until they are ready

to listen. If children need help, ask them to turn to a friend. This gives children the responsibility

of listening and the opportunity to be helpful.

If you would like to increase your affirmations:

∿ Choose three affirmations from page 28. Write them on a sticky note and place it in a spot

you will notice. Throughout the day, challenge yourself to use each affirmation at least once.

The Power of Repeated Reading in Small-Group Instruction © 2008 by Wendie Bramwell & Brooke Graham Doyle • Scholastic Professional

2)

TEACHER REFLECTION Sheet 2

TEACHER REFLECTION SHEET 3: Schedule

The Power of Repeated Reading in Small-Group Instruction © 2008 by Wendie Bramwell & Brooke Graham Doyle • Scholastic Professional

The purpose of this sheet is to help you become aware of and understand the reasons you are following your current schedule. Sometimes teachers get stuck. They don't have an opportunity to reflect on their current practice and make fresh determinations on how they want their classroom to work. Your goal is to find ways of implementing small groups and repeated readings in your classroom. In order to do this, you will need to find the time in your schedule for small groups to meet and read.

Check In

1. Use the form on page 2 to write down your weekly schedule and blocks of times you dedicate to each activity.

2. Using a highlighter, identify times in your schedule when you have some flexibility.

3. Over a three-week period, experiment with trying different configurations of small-group sessions. Remember, if you have adults who can help, it is possible to have two or even three groups listening to the story at the same time.

4. At the end of your experimental period, set up a routine and schedule that you can share with families and volunteers. Try to keep to the schedule.

1

Weekly Schedule

Monday	Tuesday	Wednesday	Thursday	Friday
A.M.	A.M.	A.M.	A.M.	A.M.
Lunch Break	Lunch Break	Lunch Break	Lunch Break	Lunch Break
P.M.	P.M.	P.M.	P.M.	P.M.

Monday	Tuesday	Wednesday	Thursday	Friday
A.M.	A.M.	A.M.	A.M.	A.M.
Lunch Break	Lunch Break	Lunch Break	Lunch Break	Lunch Break
P.M.	P.M.	P.M.	P.M.	P.M.

2

The Power of Repeated Reading in Small-Group Instruction © 2008 by Wendie Bramwell & Brooke Graham Doyle • Scholastic Professional

TEACHER REFLECTION Sheet 3

TEACHER REFLECTION SHEET 4: Classroom Climate

The purpose of this reflection is to help improve the climate in your classroom.

Reflect

Take a moment and imagine the atmosphere you would like to have throughout the day in your classroom. What words describe the climate? Visualize how you would like the day to flow and how children would behave. What roles are children assuming? Envision yourself as a facilitator of this classroom. How are you contributing to the improved climate?

Our language and attention play a significant role in encouraging or discouraging behaviors. For example, you may not realize that you are spending a good deal of energy, attention, and language solving children's problems for them. When you can objectively analyze where your time, energy, and attention are concentrated, you can redirect it towards behaviors that improve the climate.

Think about the current state of your classroom and focus on behaviors you would like to see increase. (See the list of Social-Emotional Competencies on page 35). For example, you might want to see more independent problem solving or more helping behaviors. Jot those behaviors down below.

_____

_____

_____

_____

_____

Reflect on behaviors you would like to see decrease. Perhaps it is aggression or whining.
List those behaviors.

_____

_____

_____

_____

_____

Now, prioritize the behaviors and focus on just one to increase or decrease.
Write that behavior on the line below.

_____

The Power of Repeated Reading in Small-Group Instruction © 2008 by Wendie Bramwell & Brooke Graham Doyle • Scholastic Professional

Analyze

Think about a period of the day when your chosen behavior is problematic— either you'd like to see more or less of it. Tape (audio tape is fine) that period of the day for three days during one week. Then listen and write down the words you use to deal with the target behavior. Alternatively, have a colleague observe you for this period and record the same things. For example, if the behavior you want to increase is "helping," you might record the following:

- *Sandra, please help Josh erase the board.*
- *I need someone to clean up the block area.*
- *Thank you, Celina, for helping Ms. Echeverria carry the books to the library.*
- *Where is my line leader?*

_____

_____

_____

_____

Brainstorming

Look over the notes on your language. Think about how your language and attention can increase or decrease the chosen behavior. Jot down a few ideas or phrases for you to use to improve your classroom climate. Decreasing unwanted behaviors may seem more difficult. Remember the power of ignoring an undesirable behavior, if appropriate, and attending to and/or praising the complementary desirable behavior.

Example:

- *I will assign more classroom jobs and incorporate these into the daily routine—e.g., line leader, board eraser. I will assign these in pairs where possible.*
- *I will praise any spontaneous helping behavior verbally and nonverbally. "Wow, Katerina! You really helped Max with his art project. That was really kind of you." "I like how you are helping each other understand the directions. It was confusing at first, but now it makes sense."*
- *When children ask me for help, whenever possible I will redirect them to ask a peer. I will praise the peer for helping and the child for handling it himself.*

_____

_____

_____

_____

Starting a Change

- Visualize your classroom with the classroom climate you desire. See yourself as an important component of that atmosphere.
- Pick one idea from your list to try for two days at a time to alter the chosen behavior.
- After you have tried each behavior for two days, retape yourself or invite your colleague back to observe again.
- See what changes are still needed and brainstorm ideas for those.

The Power of Repeated Reading in Small-Group Instruction © 2008 by Wendie Bramwell & Brooke Graham Doyle • Scholastic Professional

notes

A NOTE ABOUT USING CHILDREN'S LITERATURE WITH DIALOGIC READING

There are no set criteria for what makes books work well with dialogic reading since an important piece of the success of the strategy has to do with the engagement of the teacher. If a teacher loves a book, that emotion will come across to the children and they are more likely to become engaged. In addition, if the teacher enjoys the story, she will be more likely to follow through with the repeated reading of the book. However, some of the following characteristics of stories make it easier to practice the questioning strategy of dialogic reading:

★ Stories with repeated refrains (*Where the Wild Things Are, Gingerbread Baby, The Story of Ferdinand*)

★ Stories with strong emotional content (*Jamaica's Find, A Day's Work, Mean Soup*)

★ Stories with illustrations that enhance the meaning of the words (*Stellaluna, Lilly's Purple Plastic Purse*)

★ Stories that connect to the experiences and feelings of children (*Ramona the Pest, Enemy Pie, Will I Have a Friend?*)

We encourage you to select books that reflect the experiences of the children in your classroom. There are more and more outstanding books that portray children and situations in culturally sensitive and relevant contexts. Several of those are listed in the References (*Suki's Kimono, A Day's Work, Angel Child, Dragon Child, The Day of Ahmed's Secret*). More information about selecting stories can be found in Chapter 1 on page 22 (Strategies for Selecting Stories).

REFERENCES

Children's Literature Cited

Aliki. (1984). *Feelings*. New York: William Morrow and Company.

> Clear illustrations and whimsical situations provide the opportunity to discuss and explore feelings with children.

Bourgeois, P. (1997). *Franklin's new friend*. New York: Scholastic.

> Initially, Franklin is afraid of Moose, his new neighbor, because of his size, but he soon realizes that despite their differences, he has made a new friend.

Brett, J. (1999). *Gingerbread baby*. New York: Putnam.

> The traditional tale of the gingerbread man takes a twist with this version of the story, enhanced with playful illustrations, a revised, repeated refrain, and a surprise ending.

Brown, M. W. (1947). *Goodnight moon*. New York: Harper and Row.

> A simple, engaging telling of a nighttime ritual has enchanted readers for decades with its bold, primary colors, tiny hidden mouse and the quiet old lady whispering "hush."

Browne, A. (2006). *Silly Billy*. Cambridge, MA: Candlewick Press.

> Billy's parents present him with a set of Guatemalan worry dolls to help him work out his numerous worries, but Billy worries that he has overburdened the dolls with his concerns.

Bunting, E. (1994). *A day's work*. Boston: Houghton Mifflin.

> Francisco, a young Mexican-American boy, tries to help his abuelo, his grandfather, find work. Francisco discovers that even though his abuelo cannot speak English, his grandfather has something even more valuable to teach about telling the truth.

Burton, V. L. (1939). *Mike Mulligan and his steam shovel*. Boston: Houghton Mifflin.

> Mike Mulligan and Mary Anne, his steam shovel, seem to have outlived their usefulness, but with the help of a little boy and a heated contest, they find a perfect way to continue to be of use to the town.

Cain, B. (2001). *Double-dip feelings: Stories to help children understand emotions*. Washington, D.C: Magination Press.

> A series of familiar situations illustrate the uncomfortable experience of having two feelings at the same time.

Cain, J. (2000). *The way I feel*. Seattle: Parenting Press.

> Illustrations and rhyming text portray children experiencing a range of emotions, including frustration, shyness, jealousy, and pride.

Cannon, J. (1993). *Stellaluna*. San Diego: Harcourt Brace.

> A baby bat, Stellaluna, falls headfirst into a bird's nest and is raised like a bird until she is reunited with her mother.

Carle, E. (1969). *The very hungry caterpillar*. New York: Philomel.

> The hungry little caterpillar eats his way through a large quantity of different types of food until he forms a cocoon and goes to sleep.

children's

Carr, J. (1995). *Dark day, light night*. New York: Hyperion.

'Manda's aunt Ruby helps her to deal with some angry feelings by makings lists of all the things that they like in the world.

Cleary, B. (1968). *Ramona the pest*. New York: William Morrow.

Ramona is thrilled with all the new things to see and do in kindergarten, but her curiosity and eagerness to be noticed sometimes lead her into difficulties.

Cohen, M. (1967). *Will I have a friend?* New York: Macmillan.

Jim is worried about his first day of school, but his worries are forgotten when he makes a new friend.

Everitt, B. (1992). *Mean soup*. San Diego: Harcourt Brace.

A thoughtful mother coaches her son through the frustration and anger of a bad day by stirring the feelings into a soup.

Falwell, C. (2001). *David's drawings*. New York: Lee and Low Books.

David's shyness does not prevent him from using his creativity to find a way for several children to work together to draw a beautiful picture of a tree.

Fox, M. (1985). *Wilfrid Gordon McDonald Partridge*. Brooklyn: Kane/Miller.

A young boy learns to understand what memory is, and then helps his friend find her memory in a sensitive and creative way.

Freeman, D. (1978). *A pocket for Corduroy*. New York: Viking.

Corduroy, a toy bear, gets lost in a Laundromat when he searches for a pocket for his pair of overalls.

Havill, J. (1986). *Jamaica's find*. Boston: Houghton Mifflin.

Jamaica struggles with her decision to take home a stuffed dog she finds in the park rather than turn it into the lost and found.

Heide, F. P. & Gilliland, J. H. (1990). *The day of Ahmed's secret*. New York: Scholastic.

Ahmed has a secret, but before he reveals it to his family, he fulfills his responsibility of delivering heavy bottles of cooking gas throughout the neighborhood.

Henkes, K. (1996). *Lilly's purple plastic purse*. New York: HarperCollins.

Lilly loves everything about school, especially her teacher, but when he asks her to wait before showing her new purse, she does something she later regrets.

Henkes, K. (1993). *Chrysanthemum*. New York: Scholastic.

Chrysanthemum loves her name, until she starts going to school and the other children make fun of it.

Henkes, K. (1988). *Chester's way.* New York: Greenwillow Books.

Chester and Wilson share the same exact way of doing things, until Lilly moves into the neighborhood and shows them that new ways can be just as good.

Hoban, R. (1968). *A birthday for Frances.* New York: Harper and Row.

Frances's little sister, Gloria, is about to celebrate her birthday. Frances fluctuates between feeling generous and feeling jealous.

Hoffman, M. (1991). *Amazing Grace.* New York: Dial for Young Readers.

Grace is not deterred from achieving her dream of playing Peter Pan in the school play by discouraging and hurtful comments from her classmates.

Kroll, S. (1976). *That makes me mad.* New York: Pantheon.

A little girl gets mad at a lot of things in her daily life but is comforted when she explains her feelings to her mother and her mother understands.

Leaf, M. (1936). *The story of Ferdinand.* New York: Penguin Putnam.

Ferdinand the bull loves to sit and smell the flowers. He is not the fierce and snorting, stomping bull that everyone expects, until he is stung by a bee.

Lionni, L. (1963). *Swimmy.* New York: Random House.

Swimmy devises a cooperative way of helping a group of little fish who are afraid to swim in the ocean because of the big fish that might eat them.

Lionni, L. (1967). *Frederick.* New York: Pantheon.

Frederick sits on the stone wall gathering words while the other mice work hard to gather food for the winter. Though they resent it at the time, they come to appreciate Frederick's contribution during the dreary winter days.

Lionni, L. (1970). *Fish is fish.* New York: Pantheon.

Fish and Frog are inseparable friends, but when frog leaves the pond to explore and Fish follows him, Fish discovers that staying in the pond is the best option for him.

McCloskey, R. (1948). *Blueberries for Sal.* New York: Viking Press.

While eating blueberries, Little Sal and Little Bear almost end up with the other's mother.

McGovern, A. (1967). *Too much noise.* New York: Houghton Mifflin.

Peter becomes annoyed by the noises he hears in his house but quickly learns to appreciate them after following the advice of the village wise man.

Mosel, A. (1968). *Tikki Tikki Tembo.* New York: Holt, Rinehart, and Winston.

Chang desperately tries to bring help to his older brother who has fallen into the well, but his brother's very long name makes it difficult for Chang to deliver his message.

children's

Munson, D. (2000). *Enemy pie.* San Francisco: Chronicle Books.

A clever and thoughtful father helps his young child discover that the way to get rid of an enemy is to turn him into a friend.

Rey, M. & Rey, H. A. (1999). *Curious George at the parade.* Boston: Houghton Mifflin.

The holiday parade is the setting for Curious George to follow his curiosity and create chaos for those around him.

Robberecht, T. (2003). *Angry dragon.* Boston: Houghton Mifflin.

An angry young boy becomes a destructive dragon, spitting angry words, but he is transformed back to a boy by his parents' love.

Rosa-Casanova, S. (1997). *Mama Provi and the pot of rice.* New York: Simon Schuster.

When her granddaughter becomes ill, Mama Provi makes her a pot of chicken and rice, but Mama Provi only knows how to cook meals for dozens of people. She solves her problem with the help of her friendly neighbors.

Sendak, M. (1963). *Where the wild things are.* New York: HarperCollins.

Max makes mischief, sails away, tames the wild things, and returns home in time for supper.

Seuss, D. (1960). *Green eggs and ham.* New York: Random House.

The classic story of Sam trying to persuade his friend to eat green eggs and ham with his classic plea of "try it, you'll like it."

Surat, M. (1983). *Angel child, dragon child.* New York: Scholastic.

Ut faces taunting and teasing from her classmates because of her language and her clothes but strives to be an angel child rather than a dragon child.

Tresselt, A. (1964). *The Mitten.* New York: Lothrop, Lee & Shepherd.

The tiny mouse tries to share the warm space she has found in a lost mitten, but her generosity leads to problems when the mitten bursts open because of overcrowding.

Uegaki, C. (2005). *Suki's kimono.* Tonawanda, NY: Kids Can Press.

Suki's sisters are embarrassed on the first day of school when Suki proudly wears a kimono given to her by her grandmother.

Vail, R. (2002). *Sometimes I'm a bombaloo.* New York: Scholastic.

Katie feels angry and out of control, but her mother helps her to calm down and be herself again.

Viorst, J. (1972). *Alexander and the terrible, horrible, no good, very bad day.* New York: Atheneum.

Everything that possibly can go wrong goes wrong for Alexander, but he is reminded that everyone has a bad day from time to time.

Wells, R. (1973). *Noisy Nora.* New York: Dial Press.

Nora goes to great lengths to get the attention of her parents who are busy with the new baby and her older sister.

PROFESSIONAL LITERATURE CITED

Applebee, A., Langer, J., & Mullis, I. (1988). *Who reads best? Factors related to reading achievement in grades 3, 7, and 11.* Princeton, NJ: Educational Testing Service.

Arnold, D. H., Lonigan, C. J., Whitehurst, G. J., & Epstein, J. N. (1994). Accelerating language development through picture book reading: Replication and extension to a videotape training format. *Journal of Educational Psychology, 86*, 235–243.

Blair, C. (2002). School readiness: Integrating cognition and emotion in a neurobiological conceptualization of children's functioning at school entry. *American Psychologist, 57,* 111–127.

Bramwell, W., & Doyle, B. (2005). Building relationships through shared reading: Learning social and emotional skills with favorite books. *Children and Families, 19,* 28–32.

Casas, P. (2001). *Toward the ABCs: Building a healthy social and emotional foundation for learning and living.* Chicago: Ounce of Prevention.

Chow, B. W. Y., & McBride-Chang, C. (2003). Promoting language and literacy development through parent-child reading in Hong Kong preschoolers. *Early Education and Development, 14,* 233–248.

Committee for Children. (2002). *Second step: A violence prevention curriculum* (3rd ed.). Seattle: Committee for Children.

Committee for Children. (2004). *Woven word: Early literacy for life.* Seattle: Committee for Children.

Crain-Thoresen, C., & Dale, P. S. (1992). Do early talkers become early readers? Linguistic precocity, preschool language, and emergent literacy. *Developmental Psychology, 28,* 421–428.

Crain-Thoreson, C., & Dale, P. S. (1999). Enhancing linguistic performance: Parents and teachers as book reading partners for children with language delays. *Topics in Early Childhood Special Education, 16,* 213–235.

Dale, P. S., Crain-Thoreson, C., Notari-Syverson, A., & Cole, K. (1996). Parent-child book reading as an intervention technique for young children with language delays. *Topics in Early Childhood Special Education, 16,* 213– 235.

Denham, S. A. (1998). *Emotional development in young children.* New York: Guilford.

DeTemple, J. M. (2001). Parents and children reading books together. In D. K. Dickinson and P. O. Tabors (Eds.), *Beginning literacy with language* (pp. 31–51). Baltimore: Paul H. Brookes.

Dickinson, D. K. (2001a). Book reading in preschool classrooms: Is recommended practice common? In D. K. Dickinson & P. O. Tabors (Eds.), *Beginning literacy with language* (pp.175–203). Baltimore: Paul H. Brookes.

Dickinson, D. K. (2001b). Putting the pieces together: Impact of preschool on children's language and literacy development in kindergarten. In D. K. Dickinson & P. O. Tabors (Eds.), *Beginning literacy with language* (pp. 257–287). Baltimore: Paul H. Brookes.

Dickinson, D. K., & Smith, M. W. (1994). Long-term effects of preschool teachers' book readings on low-income children's vocabulary and story comprehension. *Reading Research Quarterly, 29*, 104–122.

Elias, M. J. (2003). Academic and social-emotional learning. *Educational Practices, 11*, 1–31.

Elley, W. B. (1989). Vocabulary acquisition from listening to stories. *Reading Research Quarterly, 24*, 174–187.

Fielding-Barnsley, R., & Purdie, N. (2003). Early intervention in the home for children at risk of reading failure. *Support for Learning, 18*, 77–82.

Hargrave, A. C., & Senechal, M. (2000). A book reading intervention with preschool children who have limited vocabularies: The benefits of regular reading and dialogic reading. *Early Childhood Research Quarterly, 15*, 75– 90.

Hart, B., & Risley, T. (1995). *Meaningful differences in the everyday experiences of young American children.* Baltimore: Paul H. Brookes.

Heubner, C. E. (2000). Promoting toddlers' language development through community-based intervention. *Journal of Applied Developmental Psychology, 21*, 513–535.

Kohn, A. (2001). Five reasons to stop saying "Good job!" *Young Children, 56*, 24–28.

Lonigan, C. J., & Whitehurst, G. J. (1998). Relative efficacy of parent and teacher involvement in a shared-reading intervention for preschool children from low-income backgrounds. *Early Childhood Research Quarterly, 13*, 263–290.

Meltz, B. F. (2004, September 2). If you really want to know, do more than ask "How was your day?" *Boston Globe.* Retrieved from http://www.boston.com/yourlife/family/articles/2004/09/02/.

Merryman, C. (2007, March). Ten ways to make mealtime more fun. *Family Fun*, 66.

McKeown, M. G., & Beck, I. L. (2003). Taking advantage of real-alouds to help children make sense of decontextualized language. In A. van Kleeck, S. A. Stahl, & E. B. Bauer (Eds.), *On reading books to children: Parents and teachers* (pp. 159–176). Mahwah, NJ: Erlbaum.

McNeill, J. H., & Fowler, S. A. (1999). Let's talk: Encouraging mother-child conversations during story reading. *Journal of Early Intervention, 22,* 51–69.

Morrow, L. M. (1997). *Literacy development in the early years: Helping children read and write.* Needham Heights, MA: Allyn & Bacon.

Morrow, L. M., & Smith, J. K. (1990). The effects of group size on interactive storybook reading. *Reading Research Quarterly, 25,* 213–231.

Nicholson, C. (2007, March 26). Beyond IQ: Youngsters who can focus on the task at hand do better in math. *Scientific American.* Retrieved from http://www.sciam.com/article/id/beyond-iq-kids-who-can-focus-on-task-do-better-math/SID/mail.

Paley, V. G. (1992). *You can't say you can't play.* Cambridge, MA: Harvard University Press.

Pappas, C. C. (1991). Fostering full access to literacy by including information books. *Language Arts, 68,* 449–462.

Phillips, G. & McNaughton, S. (1990). The practice of storybook reading to preschool children in mainstream New Zealand families. *Reading Research Quarterly, 25,* 196–212.

Raver, C. C. (2002). Emotions matter: Making the case for the role of young children's emotional development for early school readiness. *Social Policy Report, 16,* 3–19.

Shartrand, A., Weiss, H., Kreider, H., & Lopez, M. (1997). *New skills for new schools: Preparing teachers in family involvement.* Derby, PA: Diane Publishing.

Shonkoff, J. P., & Phillips, D. A. (2000). *From neurons to neighborhoods: The science of early childhood development.* Washington, DC: National Academy Press.

Valdez-Menchaca, M. C., & Whitehurst, G. J. (1992). Accelerating language development through picture-book reading: A systematic extension to Mexican day care. *Developmental Psychology, 28,* 1106–1114.

Vygotsky, L. S. (1978). *Mind in society: The development of psychological mental processes.* Cambridge, MA: Harvard University Press.

Wasik, B. A., & Bond, M. A. (2001). Beyond the pages of a book: Interactive book reading and language development in preschool classrooms. *Journal of Educational Psychology, 93,* 243–250.

Webster, L. (2007). Transcription of dialogic reading session.

Whitehurst, G. J., Falco, F. L., Lonigan, C. J., Fischel, J. E., DeBarysche, B. D., Valdez-Menchaca, M. C., et al. (1988). Accelerating language development through picture book reading. *Developmental Psychology, 24,* 552–559.

REFERENCES Professional Literature Cited

professional

Whitehurst, G. J., Arnold, D. S., Epstein, J. N., Angell, A. L., Smith, M., & Fischel, J. E. (1994). A picture book reading intervention in day care and home for children from low-income families. *Developmental Psychology, 30*, 679–689.

Whitehust, G. J., Epstein, J. N., Angell, A. L., Payne, A. C., Crone, D. A., & Fischel, J. E. (1994). Outcomes of an emergent literacy intervention in Head Start. *Journal of Educational Psychology, 86*, 542–555.

Whitehurst, G. J., Zevenbergen, A. A., Crone, D. A., Schultz, M. D., Velting, O. N., & Fischel, J. E. (1999). Outcomes of an emergent literacy intervention from Head Start through second grade. *Journal of Educational Psychology, 91*, 261–272.

Zevenbergen, A. A., Whitehurst, G. J., & Zevenbergen, J. A. (2003). Effects of a shared-reading intervention on the inclusion of evaluative devices in narratives of children from low-income families. *Journal of Applied Developmental Psychology, 24*, 1–15.

Zins, J. E. (2001). Examining opportunities and challenges for school-based prevention and promotion: Social and emotional learning as exemplar. *The Journal of Primary Prevention, 21*, 441–446.

Zins, J., Bloodworth, M., Weissberg, R., & Walberg, H. J. (2004). The scientific base linking social and emotional learning to school success. In J. Zins, R. Weissberg, M. Wang, & H. J. Walberg (Eds.), *Building academic success on social and emotional learning: What does the research say?* (pp.1–22). New York: Teachers Press, Columbia University.